Tree Medicine
Tree Magic

Tree Medicine
Tree Magic

by Ellen Evert Hopman

Illustrations by
Diana Green

PHOENIX PUBLISHING INC.

Please Note

In the event of a medical situation readers are advised to seek the situation of a competent health professional. Many of the remedies described in this book are based on herbal tradition; they have not necessarily been empirically proven. Persons on medications prescribed by a health professional should seek advice before ingesting herbal preparations. Some of the formulas and recipes are based on research rather than personal experience. Feedback is welcomed and encouraged.

PHOENIX PUBLISHING, INC.
P.O. Box 3829
Blaine, Washington USA 98231
www.phoenixpublishing.com

Distributed in the U.K. by
ROBERT HALE LTD.
45-47 Clerkenwell Green
London EC1R 0HT

ISBN 0-919345-55-7

Cover design © Katlyn Miller 1991

Printed in the U.S.A.

By printing this book on recycled paper we have saved 48 trees.

Contents

Dedication

This book is dedicated to all our relations
who live on the Earth Mother;
to the mineral kingdom and her living soil,
to the plant kingdom and her green medicine,
to the winged ones who fill our days with song,
to the ones who swim and crawl,
to the four-leggeds who give us their lives,
to the two-leggeds who share their hearts,
to the Devas who build our world,
to the star nations,
and to the great Archangels who guide the galaxies,
I send love and gratitude in four directions.

The Great Tree

I am the Great Tree.
My roots go deep to delve the dark places.
The sound of the waters,
the compact wisdom
of the rocks,
I know their secrets.
I am committed, steadfast.
I experience joy where I stand.
I know the inexpressible glory of the moment.
I worship in faultless bliss
and I am singing.
My hair is filled with sunlight and
I feel the winds of change—
they flow through me,
I am moved but
I stay where I am.
I know my place is perfect—
this moment, this moment is
perfect.
And I am singing.
I stretch my arms to receive them,
the lives, all who come,
I offer them shelter.
They nourish me with their sweet droppings,
their leavings,
they come and go
and I stay
singing the story,
weaving the threads of
Earth and Sky, Earth and Sky, Earth and Sky and
Sky and Earth.
And I am singing.

at Temenos
July 1988

Introduction

My purpose in writing this book is twofold. First, I wish to remind the world of the beauty and poetry of the large trees that are being decimated everywhere to make room for parking lots and shopping malls, to make paper and wood products, and also through the destruction of rainforests and wildlands. My second intention is to bring to public awareness how useful natural medicines are, how easy they are to prepare, and how available they are year round in our own back yards.

I have chosen to incorporate both herbal and magical lore in this text to add to the mystery of the trees and because our ancestors would have done it that way. By keeping alive the rich body of tradition surrounding valuable trees and herbs our ancestors hoped to ensure that future generations would continue to honor and respect the healing and life sustaining virtues these trees and herbs offer.

Magic is a misunderstood art in this day of scientific rationalism, and it has been turned into a subject of derision and fear by religious bodies who claim exclusive authority over the mysteries of life and death. For me, magic is the conscious application of imagination and focused attention to bring about a desired goal through visualization. The guidelines are clear—harm others and it comes back to you. Perform a kindness, and a similar rule applies.

Modern medicine is only beginning to explore the power of visualization for enhancing the immune system and for overcoming illness. Traditional magic teaches that through visualization all aspects of life can be transformed.

Our society is beginning to appreciate the ancient remedies of our fore-mothers. In a world that pushes new foods and drugs on the public at an increasing rate, many people are starting to question the long term effects of synthetic medicines. There is evidence that our own body's defence mechanisms are being compromised.

If we are concerned about chemical pollutants in our food, air, and water, we must ask ourselves what the effect will be of the continual drugging recommended by the pharmaceutical industry. Doctors, too, are victims. They have been taught that drugs and surgery are the tools of their art. Few are aware of the precious life-strengthening powers inherent in natural foods and in plant medicines.

Our churches are undergoing a crisis as congregations dwindle and the general population either seeks new religious traditions or gives up religion altogether.

Ancient cultures were inextricably tied to the cycle of the seasons—the planting time, the period of growth, the harvest, and the fallow sleep of winter. Our society is waking up to the fact that terrestrial resources are limited and that we should pay closer attention to Mother Nature and what she is trying to tell us.

The ancient religions of Western Europe and the Americas placed an extraordinary emphasis on trees as symbols of the Divine Presence. Native American tribes based entire cultures on their uses of a particular tree. To the Northwest coast people, cedar was "Long Life Maker" and "Rich Woman Maker" because it supplied canoes, houses, carvings, basket materials, matting, clothing, rope, and medicine. Similarly, our pre-Christian European ancestors attributed spiritual powers to trees and spun elaborate traditions around them.

Archaeology has provided us with evidence of the powerful religious significance of trees to our early kindred. Boughs of oak and sprays of mistletoe have been found in ancient coffins. Celtic place names sometimes incorporate the word Nemeton (sacred grove). Nanterre in France was once called Nemetodurum. Vaison (Vauduse) was called Nemeton. We find Nemetacum in northeast Gaul, and Nemtobriga in Spanish Galicia. Nottinghampshire was known as Vernemeton in Roman days, and Medionemeton was located near the Antonine Wall in Scotland.

Eyewitness accounts state that during the Roman occupation of Britain and Gaul the druids used groves of trees for their ceremonies because they believed that it was a sacrilege to worship in man-made structures. We know, too, that assemblies were held under the canopies of ash and yew trees and that it was forbidden to harm those trees in any way.

There are ancient Gaulish altars that have the image of a tree as their only decoration. Sometimes the god Erriapus is shown emerging from the foliage. The name of the Gaulish god Olloudios meant "Great Tree."

The famous Gundestrup cauldron of Denmark shows warriors in an enigmatic relationship to a fallen tree. Some say the tree is carried by them impaled on their spears. As it is a sacrificial scene that is depicted, perhaps the fallen tree symbolizes a life "cut down?" Large and deep wells were sometimes dug into which offerings were thrown—sometimes the offering was an entire tree!

At his death the Welsh god Lleu transformed himself into an eagle and took refuge in the branches of an oak. This mighty tree could neither be flooded by rain nor burned by fire. In this tree Lleu suffered many tests and trials. Similarly, the Germanic god Odin was said to have endured great suffering in the ash tree Yggdrasil as he underwent a voluntary self-sacrifice and discovered runes. Our present Christian tradition holds that the son of God died on a tree for the good of humanity. And the Lord Buddha was said to have achieved enlightenment while meditating under a tree.

From the apple trees of Avalon, to the golden apples of the garden of the Hesperides, we have stories of sacred trees whose magical fruits are often the goal of heroic legends.

In Scott's Gaelic, a great hero is often complemented by comparing him to a mighty tree. "Craobh a b'airde de n'abhall thu'." (You are the tallest tree in the orchard.) An early Irish heroine is named Caer Ibormeith (Yewberry).

In this book I have tried to bring back to life the spiritual, practical, and medical traditions developed by our ancestors, the celebrants of the trees.

The Seneca Tradition

From time to time I will make references to the Seneca tradition. The Seneca are a northeast American woodland people who have lived in harmony with nature for thousands of years. Originally called "the people of the great hill," they were one of the original five nations of the Iroquois confederacy.

As Americans we are indebted to the many who helped frame our constitution, but the idea for the document seems to have come from the Iroquois confederacy. According to one tradition, a Peacemaker appeared among the nations at a time of great intertribal bloodshed and terror. His mission was to unite the people under the Great Law of Peace. Having convinced each tribe that the others would join if they did, he led the tribal leaders in a ceremony. He unearthed a "tree of the long leaves" (a White Pine) and had the people throw their weapons into the hole so that the underground rivers could carry away any bad thoughts contained in them. He then re-planted the tree.

He then taught the people to meet under the protection of the tree. Pine needles grow in clusters of five and this repre-sented the individual families. Each branch symbolized a clan and all the clans were joined to one trunk that was rooted firmly in the earth and that reached for the sky.

At the top of the tree the Peacemaker placed an eagle (the-one-who-sees-far) to warn the chiefs of any approaching danger. The tree was said to have four great roots growing north, east, south, and west. People of every nation were in-vited to follow these roots to the source and to sit with the Iroquois under the Great Tree of Peace.

Some Herbal Basics

Flower Essences

Flower essences are made by placing newly opened flowers in a crystal bowl, covering them with water, and allowing them to be exposed to full sunlight on a cloudless day for four full hours. After straining, the water is preserved by mixing with natural brandy (without artificial colors or flavors—available in liquor stores), about forty percent of the total volume. It is stored in brown glass containers. This "Mother Tincture" is then diluted with water—two drops per one ounce of water. The dose is four drops, four times a day, under the tongue, but not with meals.

Infusions

(For leaves and flowers.) Bring springwater to a boil in a non-aluminum pot. Remove it from the stove. Place two tea-spoons of the herb in the water for each cup boiled. Steep for twenty to forty-five minutes. Strain and store for up to a week in airtight containers under refrigeration. The dose is generally one quarter cup, four times per day.

Decoctions

(For roots, twigs and barks.) Place two teaspoons of plant

matter for each cup of water into a non-aluminum pot with a good lid. Simmer for about twenty minutes, then strain and store in an airtight container, under refrigeration, for up to a week. The dose is one quarter cup, four times a day.

Tinctures

The best tinctures are made by gathering fresh roots, barks, and leaves or flowers, although dried herbs can be used if necessary. Grind the herbs with a mortar and pestle, or use a blender. Cover them lightly with good quality vodka, whiskey, or grain alcohol, and leave them in an airtight glass container in a dark place for twenty-one days, shaking them from time to time. When the tincture is mature, add a little glycerine (about two tablespoons per quart) and some pure spring water (about ten percent of the total volume). Strain and store the fluid in amber glass jars or in tightly closed containers in a dark place.

Salves

A simple salve can be made by simmering leaves or husks of the nut (as indicated) in cold pressed olive oil for about twenty minutes. Beeswax is simultaneously simmered and, when both preparations reach the same temperature, they are poured together, stirred, strained, and stored in sterilized glass jars. Use about four tablespoons of beeswax for each cup of oil.

Dosages

Unless otherwise indicated, all dosages given are for adults. Children receive half the amount and babies one quarter the amount. Newborns can be treated by allowing the mother to drink the indicated remedy and pass it through her breast milk.

Gathering Tree Medicines

Tree leaves are generally gathered in spring or early summer. By midsummer the trees have produced high levels of insecticide to repel bugs and the green plant materials may be irritating to human tissue. When bark is gathered it is generally peeled and dried. The inner bark (cambrium) and the bark of the root have medicinal properties. Try to gather bark from a branch or from the roots of a felled tree. It is exceptionally bad karma to pull the bark off the trunk of a living tree! Never "girdle" a tree by cutting bark in a circular ring around it. This will kill the tree.

Homeopathy

Homeopathy is a system of medicine that recognizes that diseases are complexes of symptoms that involve the mental, emotional, and physical aspects of a person. The remedies are made by repeated dilution and agitation of alcoholic tinctures from plants and some mineral and animal products. Homeopathic remedies can be purchased from health food stores and homeopathic pharmaceutical firms. (See the sources and resources section at the end of this book.) Homeopathic remedies are non-toxic, available over the counter, and approved by the FDA.

In winter, when there is but one green leaf
for many rods, what warm content is in them!
They are not rude,
but tender even in the severest cold.
Their nakedness is their defense....
The trees have come down to the bank
to see the river go by.
— Henry David Thoreau

White Oak

Oak

Faerie-folks are in Old Oaks

THE WHITE OAK *(Quercus alba)*
*This is a slow growing, open branched native of the eastern U.S.
which grows to a height of ninety feet. It produces purplish-red
leaves in the fall which are elliptical, four to nine inches long,
and two to five inches wide. The leaves have five to nine lobes.
They are widest beyond the middle and taper off at the base.
The bark is light gray, and shallowly fissured in broad, scaly
plates which are often loose. The acorns are about an inch
long, egg-shaped, and one quarter enclosed is a shallow cup. It
favors moist, well drained soils, and will grow in altitudes up to
5500 feet from southern Ontario and east central Minnesota to
eastern Texas, Main and northern Florida. The bark and leaves
are used medicinally.*

THE ENGLISH OAK *(Quercus robur)*
*A European, African, and west Asian tree with a broad head
and a short trunk. It grows to eighty feet. In England it may live
a thousand years or more. The leaves are two to five inches
long, and one and a quarter to two and a half inches wide, with
six to fourteen shallow rounded lobes near the short stalked
base. The bark is dark gray with deep and irregular furrows. The
acorns are about one inch long, egg shaped, and one third
enclosed by a half round cup. It favors moist soil on the edge of
roads and forests. This tree has been introduced to southeastern
Canada and northeastern United States, but cold injury often
results at latitudes north of Boston. The bark is used medicinally.*

THE NORTHERN RED OAK *(Quercus rubra)*
*A common American tree, native to central and northeast
North America. It is one of the fastest growing oaks. It's shape
is pyramidal in the sapling stage but it becomes rounded with
age. The leaves are red in autumn, four to nine inches long,
three to six inches wide, elliptical, with seven to eleven shallow
wavy lobes and a few irregular bristle-tipped teeth. The bark is
gray or black and roughly furrowed with scaly ridges. The inner
bark is reddish. The acorns are five eighths to one and an*

*eighth inches long, egg shaped, and less than one third enclosed
in a broad, reddish, blunt cup that has tightly overlapping
scales. It favors moist, sandy, rocky, loamy, and clay soils. Its
range is from western Ontario to Cape Breton Island, and
south to Georgia and eastern Oklahoma. It grows in altitudes
to 5500 feet in the south.*

THE BLACK OAK *(Quercus velutina)*
*A large North American oak that has an exceptionally long
taproot. The powdered inner bark yields Quercitron which
produces a buff, gold, or orange dye. Its leaves turn red in
autumn, are four to nine inches long and three to five inches
wide, elliptical, narrow, with seven to nine lobes (both shallow
and deep), and they end in bristle-tipped teeth. It grows to a
height of eighty feet. The bark is gray and smooth on young
trees, and it is black, thick, and furrowed with rough deep ridges
on older trees. The inner bark is yellow or orange and has a bitter taste. The acorns are five eighths to three quarter inches
long, elliptical, and half enclosed by a thick cup which is nar-
rowed at its base and has a fringe of rust colored, hairy scales.
It favors dry, sandy, rocky, or clay soils. Its range is from
southern Ontario to southeastern Minnesota, and central Texas
east to Maine and northwestern Florida.*

I am blessed to be living in an oak forest in western Massachusetts. They line my driveway and stand outside my
kitchen door. It is to them that I owe the inspiration for this
book.

As a professional herbalist, I maintain several small
patches of medicinal herbs around my house. My clients and
students are often directed to local supermarkets and her-
bariums to buy healing herbs and this can be a frustrating
experience. Growing conditions in many areas are such that
winter will force people to depend on commercial estab-
lishments unless they have dried herbs from a summer garden.
What a joy to discover that certain trees, such as the oak, are
available year round.

Several years ago my love of Celtic music and dance led me
to the study of Celtic mysticism. I quickly became fascinated by
the druids, the legendary poet-priests of pre-Christian
Europe. The available literature yielded an important insight:
because the Celts lived as far south as Portugal and Spain, and

as far east as Russia, almost anyone with European blood is bound to have Celtic ancestors. This made them kin of mine and therefore worthy of serious study.

When most of us think of the druids one image stands out— the vision of the sacred grove of oaks. Why did our ancestors value this tree so highly? Could it be that trees which were extremely valuable for survival became associated with the power of the gods? Our ancestors were also sensitive to the spiritual qualities that could be felt in the presence of an oak tree.

One day while in meditation, I was inspired to get up and hug a nearby tree. It occurred to me with overwhelming certainty that this tree was the "royal protector" of the surrounding area. It was standing sentinel, protecting local vegetation and animals, and only when I lifted my eyes to its branches did I realize that this mighty spirit was an oak.

The word druid may have been derived from the Celtic derw (oak), and ydd (a part of), which combine to form Derwydd, the ancient term for the Celtic priest class. The druids may have chosen oak as their favorite tree because of its strength and endurance. This tree has roots that are at least as deep as its branches are high, with a strong, stout trunk to channel the forces of earth and sky. Oaks are often struck by lightning and survive, and thus symbolize spirituality which is well grounded, but that reaches for the heights.

Oaks also have an honored place in the hearts and minds of the people of Britain—the island was once covered with vast oak forests. We know that Arthur's Round Table was made from the single slab of an oak tree. Trees of up to thirty-six feet in diameter have been recorded as growing in British soil.

Avoid oaks during thunderstorms as they tend to draw lightning.

Practical Uses

The oak is considered the finest building material because it is strong and flexible. It is a very dense hardwood and is unsurpassed as a heating fuel. Oak bark is also rich in tannic acid and this makes it ideal for tanning hides.

Oak bark mixed with additives produces various dyes for

cloth. Iron salts added to oak bark makes a black dye, alum salts a brown, and tin salts or zinc salts a yellow. The inner bark of the Black Oak will create yellow on alum mordanted wool, gold with the addition of chrome, and olive green with copperas. Silk will dye orange. With the addition of copperas, the English Oak colors wool black.

Acorns were, until recently, a prime fodder for pigs, and were also used as a staple food for humans in times of famine. Most acorns are extremely bitter; they need to be leached in a running stream for days, or boiled repeatedly in hot water, before they can be eaten as nuts or ground into flour. Their nutritional components are 6.3 percent water, 5.2 percent protein, 43 percent fat, and 45 percent carbohydrate. The acorns of the White Oak are the most palatable.

 ## Herbal Uses

Oaks are known for astringent tonics. This means they will tend to shrink, tone, and heal tissues. A tea made from the bark is used as an enema for hemorrhoids or as a douche for vaginitis. It will benefit bloody urine, stop internal hemorrhages, reduce fevers, and soothe sore throats. Oak bark tea may be used internally and externally to shrink varicose veins, and as a wash for sores and skin irritations. It has been used as a hair rinse to stop hair loss and dandruff.

Culpeper advises using an infusion of the leaves for douching and a tea of the bark to check diarrhea. Sebastion Kniepp says a cloth dipped into a decoction of the fresh or dried bark can be wrapped around the neck to heal goiters and glandular inflammations. He also recommends a sitz-bath (four inches of tea in the bathtub) plus occasional enemas for prolapse of the rectum and fistulas, and tumors of the rectal area. The leaves and bark are used together as a dressing for burns.

The acorns and bark of the White Oak are made into a decoction and added to milk to counteract the side effects of harsh medicines, especially when the bladder has been damaged and there is blood in the urine.

White Oak bark, taken as a tea, helps clean the body of excess mucus caused by sinus congestion, post nasal drip, and lung congestion. It also improves the stomach's ability to absorb and secrete substances. Collect the bark in early spring from young branches, twigs, and the trunks of saplings.

To make the tea, place one tablespoon of bark in one pint water and simmer for ten minutes. Drink up to three cups per day. For enemas and douches, simmer one tablespoon of bark in one quart water for thirty minutes, then strain and use the fluid.

(Spiritus Glandium Quercus) and (Aqua Glandium Quercus) are homeopathic preparations made from peeled acorns and used to treat alcoholism, bad breath, constipation, diarrhea, splenic dropsy, fistula, dizziness, gout, intermittent fever, leukemia, and splenic conditions.

Dr. Edward Bach, the inventor of flower essence therapy, prescribed the flower essence of oak for those people who experience despondency and despair, yet keep on trying. These people never seem to give up hope, and are disappointed if an illness keeps them from their work. They enjoy helping others, and may overwork themselves, hiding their tiredness so as not to disturb anyone. They are patient, strong, and endowed with common sense. When healthy, they reflect perseverance, courage, and stability.

Magical Uses

Not surprisingly, there is a wealth of magical lore dealing with the oak. It is a tree ruled by the sun, associated with the element Fire, and it bestows the qualities of protection, healing, financial success, sexual potency, fertility, and general good luck.

To protect against evil, several books recommend making a cross (the symbol of balance) out of oak twigs tied together with a red ribbon. Carrying a piece of oak will offer protection.

Acorns are powerful magical tools as well. They can be placed in a window to ward off lightning, carried to prevent illness and pain, and worn as talismans of fertility, immortality, and longevity. Plant one in the dark of the moon to induce financial prosperity. Because acorns are symbolic of immortality and the continuity of life, they are especially appropriate to the Samhain or Hallowe'en season. Use them as ornaments and to decorate altars in the fall.

Oak branches were traditionally burned in midsummer fires and used to make wands and staves. Topping them with an acorn will help in fertility rituals. The working of positive magic will be enhanced if the wood for wands is gathered during the waxing moon. Be sure to leave an appropriate gift as an exchange.

To help in healing a wound, an old custom advises that you take a dressing that has been on the injured body part, sprinkle it with oil of Rue, and place it inside the hollow of an oak tree during the waning moon. The wound will be transferred through the tree to the ground and dispersed into the earth.

When gathering leaves, acorns, or branches of oak, it is fitting to honor the old custom of "feeding the oak" by pouring a libation of wine on the roots. Acorns are best gathered by day, and leaves and wood by night. Oaks should only be cut down during the waning moon. A few days before cutting the tree, take time to tell it what you are about to do. You can plant an acorn near the old tree so that the Tree Spirit will have a new home.

The Gaelic word for oak is duir from which we have made the word "door." A "door" is both a gateway and a protection from outside influences. The oak opens the door to a strong spiritual focus that is able to survive the tests and ordeals of time.

The Latin for oak is quercus from the Celtic quer (fine) and cuez (tree). The Quercus species is sacred to the Dagda, Dianus, Jupiter, Thor, Zeus, Hercules, Herne, Janus, Rhea, Cerridwen, Cernunnos, Cybele, Hecate, Pan, Erato, Bridget, Blodeuedd, and Odin. For those inclined towards the Old Religion, the burning of powdered oak bark as incense is an appropriate offering for any of these gods. Oaks are part of the sacred triad of "Oak and Ash and Thorn." The Celts were very partial to the number three, and where these three trees grew together it was said one was likely to see fairies.

Twylah Nitsch, of the Seneca tribe, in her book *Language of the Trees,* has published a nice introduction to the Native American perception of the symbolism of trees. To the Seneca indians, the oak, with its aura of reserved power, is a tree of strength—a strength that is the result of decades of steady growth. The oak conveys a sense of structure and solidity, and it symbolizes self-discipline, awareness, and high ideals.

The Seneca tribe sensed that trees could be used as tools for personal growth, and as a mirror for defining individuals. Oak people are felt to be motivators and creative thinkers with

an efficient eye for detail. They project reliability, gentle firm-
ness, and sincerity. Strong and silent, these people are
spiritually inclined and derive inner strength from taking the
time to center themselves. They trust in their intuition and
listen carefully to their inner voices.

The trees indeed have hearts.
With a certain affection the sun seems to send
its farewell ray far and level over the copses to them,
and they silently receive it with gratitude,
like a group of settlers with their children.
The pines impress me as human.
A slight vaporous cloud floats high over them,
while in the west the sun goes down apace behind glowing pines,
and golden clouds like mountains skirt the horizon.
— Henry David Thoreau

Eastern Hemlock

Pine

Evergreen Pine, the Tree of Immortality

THE EASTERN HEMLOCK, HEMLOCK SPRUCE, OR CANADA
HEMLOCK
(Tsuga canadensis = Abies canadensis = Pinus canadensis)
*A common native to the United States which can live 500 years.
The inner bark and growing shoot tips are edible. A conical
evergreen with long, slender branches that droop to the ground,
it attains a height of seventy feet and a trunk diameter of three
feet. The needles are evergreen, three eighths to five eighths of
an inch long, flat, flexible and rounded, and shiny dark green
above with two whitish narrow bands beneath. The bark is cinnamon brown and deeply furrowed with thickly scaly ridges.
The twigs are very slender and rough. The cones are five eighths
to three quarters of an inch long, elliptical, brown, and they
dangle from the end of the twig. They are made up of rounded
cone scales. The tree favors acid soil, moist, cool and shady
areas, and rocky, north facing outcrops. Its range is from
southern Ontario to eastern Minnesota, east to Cape Breton Island and northern Alabama. It grows in altitudes to 3000 feet
in the north and 5000 feet in the south.*

THE BLACK SPRUCE
(Picea mariana = Abies nigra = Pinus nigra)
*The tree has an irregular crown of slightly drooping branches
and can grow to sixty feet with a trunk diameter of twelve inches. The needles are evergreen, a quarter to five eighths of an
inch long, sharp pointed, stiff, and four angled. The color is an
ashy blue-green. The bark is gray, thin, and scaly with a yellowish inner bark. The twigs are hairy, rough, slender, and
brown. The cones are five eighths to one and a quarter inches
long, egg shaped, dull gray, and curve downward on a short
stalk. They tend to cluster near the crown of the tree. The tree
favors the wet and boggy soil of peat, clay or loam in forest
areas. It grows in altitudes to 5000 feet. The low branches take
root when deep snows force them to the ground. Native
Americans make a spruce beer by boiling the twigs and cones in*

*maple syrup. It grows from Labrador to Alaska, and south to
Michigan and Wisconsin.*

THE WHITE PINE *(Pinus strobus = Pinus alba)*
*A native of eastern North America. It attains a height of one
hundred feet or more with a trunk diameter of up to four feet.
The needles are evergreen, two and a half to five inches long,
and grow in bundles of five. The bark is gray on young trees and
becomes thickly furrowed and rough on older specimens. The
cones are five to eight inches long, narrow, and yellowish
brown. It favors well drained, sandy soil. Its range is from
southeast Manitoba to northeast Iowa, and from Newfoundland to northern Georgia. It grows from sea level to 2000
feet in the north, and to altitudes of 5000 feet in the south. The
needles can be brewed into tea.*

THE BALSAM FIR
(Abies balsamea = Terebirithine canadensis)
*This tree prefers cool, moist, mountain forests. The inner bark
is edible and the tips of young shoots can be made into a tea. It
grows into a narrow pointed spire with exceptionally fragrant
foliage. It attains a height of sixty feet and a trunk diameter of
one and a half feet. The needles are evergreen, up to one inch
long, and grow in two rows on hairy twigs. They are flat with a
rounded or notched tip, and shiny dark green above with two
whitish bands beneath. The bark is brown, thin, and smooth
when young, and later becomes scaly with resin pockets. The
cones are two to three inches long, cylindrical and deep purple,
and they grow upright on the top branches. It grows from Alber-
ta to Minnesota and northeast Iowa, and from Labrador to Virginia. In the north it grows to the timberline and in the south to
altitudes of 4000 feet. It is a favorite food tree of deer and
moose.*

This chapter was started on the day of the winter solstice—
the day that marks the end of the darkness and the return of
the light. For me, winter seems to lose its grip just after the
solstice. Certain birds and plants will reappear due to the
lengthening days. Since ancient times, this season of light has
been celebrated as the birth of the Sun God who is symbolized
by the Evergreen Pine.

So ingrained in our culture is this mystical relationship
with pine that we continue to follow the tradition of honoring

its evergreen spirit at Christmas. I was always dismayed by the deaths of millions of trees at this time of year and refused to have a Christmas tree. This year, a friend suggested I try a new tactic. Every year after Christmas there are trees left over at the tree farms and church parking lots that no one wants to buy. These trees are misshapen, or filled with "gaps," and somehow fail to conform to human esthetic taste. As a result, they are passed over and their lives are wasted.

My friend's ingenious solution is to seek out the ugliest most asymmetrical tree she can find. This tree is brought home and honored with beautiful decorations. I followed her example and found that my little misshapen tree had a natural, windswept beauty that made it truly original and deeply loved.

The rich symbolism of the pine conifers can best be understood by examining Native American beliefs. Pines were considered sacred by the native people of the Americas and central Europe. To the Iroquois, the pine symbolizes a balanced life existence. Its shape, which reaches for the sky like a pair of praying hands, suggests the search for Truth.

Pines grow in a circular shape. Circles symbolize energy cycles like the year's seasonal wheel, the motions of the planets, stars, and of life and rebirth. Pines reach a great age reminding us of the links between generations. Their wood is soft, symbolizing a strength that is gentle yet firm. The even texture of the bark reminds one of an intelligence consciously directed towards a clear purpose in life.

Pine needles grow in bundles, symbolizing strength through unity. The cones are curved, representing adaptability, while the sticky sap that holds the seeds reminds us of the importance of cohesiveness.

Pine trees carry a message of concern for future generations and a dream of peace for all beings. In bygone days, many Native American tribes would gather at a yearly congress. To commemorate these important gatherings, it was the custom to plant a pine, the tree of peace.

Practical Uses

Pine is one of the most prolific of the softwood timbers, and is used for lumber, furniture, construction, paneling, musical instruments, toys, household implements, poles, and pilings. It is an important food and shelter source for wildlife, and has an ornamental value for humans. Native Americans used pine needles for baskets and decorations, ate the nuts, and used the resin as a type of glue. Pine nuts (from the White Pine) were ground and added to soups.

The bark of the Eastern Hemlock dyes wool brown (with or without the addition of alum). Pine resin is used by violinists to condition their bows. It is also used in varnishes, sealing wax, resinous brown soaps, papier-mâché, and for brewer's pitch to coat the inside of beer casks.

Herbal Uses

Pine resins have long been used as healing agents. A type of tar that is antiseptic, expectorant, and useful for lung conditions can be obtained by distilling the resin. (Pine tar water is also given to horses with chronic coughs.) The tar can be used internally and externally both as a stimulant and as an antiseptic for skin conditions. To use the tar, mix it with ten parts of water, and allow it to decant. Pour off the liquid, add sweetening, and take two teaspoons as a dose.

Pine resin can be gathered by tapping the trees directly. Chewed, the resinous gum will soothe a sore throat, or the dried and powdered resin can be applied to a sore throat with a swab, or blown onto the back of the throat with a straw. When heated and spread on a cloth, pine resin is an excellent plaster for lung conditions, sciatica, and sore muscles.

The distilled resin yields oil of turpentine which can be applied as an external stimulant for rheumatic conditions, sprains, and bruises. Internally, the oil of turpentine will kill parasites and is useful for lung conditions. The dose for lung conditions is two to ten drops in water or herb tea. The oil is also used for horses and cattle as a deworming medicine. Turpentine for this purpose should be purchased from a reliable veterinary supply house.

Pine oil is put into ointments and liniments that are used for sciatica and skin eruptions such as eczema and psoriasis. A simple way to impart the benefits of pine to your skin is to gather fresh needles, twigs, and resinous cones and simmer them in a high quality oil (almond or olive). When strained, this makes a fragrant and healthful massage oil.

A pine bath can be of help to older people as it stimulates their skin, strengthens blood vessels, and will benefit kidney and bladder diseases. Gather small branches, sprigs, and cones, cut in pieces, and simmer for half an hour in fresh water. The decoction is strained and added to a warm bath. Follow the bath with a quick, cold water shower.

The Black Spruce is used as an antiscorbutic (prevents scurvy). As with hemlock and White Pine, Native Americans made it into a tea to prevent vitamin C deficiency. In early spring you can "graze" on the pale green, new growth that appears on hemlocks and it is delicious. It will have a lemony taste and be rich in vitamin C. The inner bark of the White Pine is boiled to make a cough remedy.

A tonic was once made on southern plantations that consisted of molasses and pine needles, a cheap and effective method to keep the slaves healthy. This vitamin and iron-rich tonic saved many lives.

The bark and twigs of the Balsam Fir are simmered with four times their weight of glycerine and honey to make a tea that will benefit kidney and bladder complaints, fevers, lung conditions, and rheumatism. The dose is one teaspoon, four times a day.

The resin from the Balsam Fir is beneficial for wounds and works well as a liniment for sore muscles and rheumatic pains.

Dr. Bach recommends pine flower essence for those who are filled with self-reproach, guilt, and despondency. It is good for people who tend to blame themselves for mistakes, their own and those of others, and for those who spend inordinate amounts of time attempting to "improve" themselves. When ill, they blame themselves for failing their family and friends, and guilt robs them of their joy in life. Such individuals will sink into depression and even despair when they are unable live up to their own high standards. In a positive or healthy state these people are willing to take responsibility for others (when appropriate), acknowledge their mistakes, and harbor great reserves of perseverance and humility. Any person displaying these characteristics will be healed and balanced by the pine flower essence.

Terebinthina (turpentine) and Terebene, volatile oils and residues left from the distillation of turpentine from pine trees, are used homeopathically to relieve chronic bronchitis, sub-acute respiratory tract infections, neurotic coughs,

singers' and speakers' sore throat, cystitis, kidney inflammations, chilblains, and conditions marked by bleeding mucous
surfaces.

The Hemlock Spruce (Abies Canadensis/Pinus Canadensis) is used homeopathically for mucous conditions that relate
to the stomach and uterus. Such conditions are accompanied
by cold, clammy skin and hands, exhaustion, and gnawing
hunger. The Black Spruce (Abies Nigra) is used to help faulty
digestion in the aged, constipation, pain in the chest, and
impaired thinking.

Magical Uses

In the world of magic, pine is valued for its associations
with fertility, purification, and immortality. It is known as a
tree of Mars, and it is representative of the elements of Earth
and Air. Its associated deities are Cybele, Venus, Attis, Pan,
Dionysus, Poseidon, Astarte, and Sylvanus.

The Spirit of the Forest is recognized in many places
throughout the world as a being who dwells in pines. The
oldest and most gnarled of trees is a likely home for this spirit,
and such a tree is known as the "King of the Forest" or the
"Grandmother Tree." Needless to say, the Forest Spirit
strongly objects to having this special tree cut down.

The most sacred high altar in Korea is situated in a pine
forest. It was to this altar of the "Spirits of the Land" that
government officials went when Korea gained independence
from Japan.

The Chinese plant pine trees on graves because they
believe them to be full of a vital force that will keep the body
from decay and that will strengthen the spirit of the departed.

Cybele, the Greek Mother Goddess of mountains and
forests was once worshipped in wild ceremonies that involved
the clashing of cymbals, loud singing, pipe playing, and burning
torches. Her devotees ran through the woods at night attack-
ing each other.

This frenzied rite commemorated Cybele's loss of Attis, a
Phrygian shepherd whom she loved. Attis was about to be
married to the princess of Pessinus when Cybele disrupted the
wedding by terrifying the guests. Attis fled to the mountains
where he wounded himself and eventually died beside a pine

tree. His soul transmigrated into the pine, and his spilled blood turned into violets that circled the tree.

Cybele petitioned Zeus to return Attis to life, but her wish was refused. Instead, Zeus ordained that his body would never decay, his hair would always grow, and his fingers would always move. Thus the Evergreen Pine became a symbol of winter and melancholy, and the violet a symbol of spring and eternal hope.

The ancient Assyrians and Chaldeans believed that the World Tree was located in the Forest of Eridhu. The Izdubar Epic, found on an ancient tablet, describes the tree as one whose seat was the center of the earth. It said that it had a root of white crystal and that its foliage was of heaven. They called it the Great Mother. This tree is believed to be a pine or possibly a cedar.

Pine is the appropriate tree to burn during the Yule and other winter rites, and its branches are used to sweep the forest floor in preparation for winter rituals. From November first to March twenty-first it is burned in the hearth to purify the home. A cross of pine branches placed before an unused fireplace keeps evil from entering. Pine branches are hung over sick beds as a preventative measure and to help the healing process. In Japan a pine branch is hung over the door to ensure joy for the occupants of the home.

Crushed and dried pine needles are mixed with juniper and cedar and burned to purify and scent the home. Pine resin can be gathered right from the tree and burned as incense to clear negative energies. The smoke also repels evil and sends the negative force back to its source.

Traditionally, pine pitch has been used to caulk ships in honor of Poseidon. It is hoped that he will then extend his magical protection to the ship.

Cones are carried as fertility charms and pine nuts are eaten for the same effect. A pine cone is gathered on midsummer's day and one seed a day is eaten to become immune to the sun's heat.

In Dionysian ceremonies, a thyrsus was carried by Dionysus (Bacchus) and his votaries. This was generally a giant fennel stalk with pine cones attached to the ends.

In Mexico, wreaths of garlic bulbs, pictures of saints, bags of herbs, stones, rocks, salt, fresh aloe plants, and pine nuts decorate the walls to protect and ensure prosperity in the home.

It is an old custom to place fresh pine boughs on a coffin during funeral rites and at burials. The evergreen symbol of immortality is a fitting salute to the departed and a consolation to the bereaved. In Orthodox Jewish funerals, the only permissible wood for a coffin is pine which is a remnant of their ancestors' regard for the Spirit of this tree.

If you plan to cut pine branches, use a sharp knife. Tell the tree what you are about to do and why, and be sure to leave a gift of coin, tobacco, or a libation as thanks.

I long for wilderness, a nature which
I can not put my foot through,
woods where the wood thrush forever sings,
where the hours are early morning ones,
and there is dew on the grass,
and the day is forever unproved....
— Henry David Thoreau

I wonder about the trees.
Why do we wish to bear
Forever the noise of these
More than another noise
So close to our dwelling place?
We suffer them by the day
Till we lose all measure of pace,
And fixity in our joys,
And acquire a listening air.
They are that that talks of going
But never gets away;
And that talks no less for knowing,
As it grows wiser and older,
That now it means to stay.
My feet tug at the floor
And my head sways to my shoulder
Sometimes when I watch trees sway,
From the window or the door.
I shall set forth for somewhere,
I shall make the reckless choice
Some day when they are in voice
And tossing so as to scare
The white clouds over them on.
I shall have less to say,
But I shall be gone.
— Robert Frost

White Ash

Ash

Supple Ash, the Unicorns' Friend

THE WHITE ASH *(Fraxinus americana)*
*Famous for providing wood for baseball bats. The tree has a
straight trunk and a dense, rounded crown of foliage. The ash
attains a height of eighty feet with a trunk diameter of two feet.
The leaves are opposite, pinnately compound, and are eight to
twelve inches long. There are five to seven leaflets that are one
and a half to five inches long and one and a quarter to two and
a half inches wide and they are paired except at the tip. The
leaves are ovate and edged with very fine teeth, and they turn
purple or yellow in the fall. The bark is dark gray with deep
diamond shaped furrows. The twigs are grayish and stout.
Purplish flowers appear in small clusters prior to the leaves. The
fruit hang in clusters of keys that are one to two inches long. It
favors hardwood forests with deep well drained loam. Its range
is from southern Ontario to eastern Minnesota and eastern
Texas, and from Cape Breton Island to northern Florida. It
grows in altitudes to 2000 feet in the north and 5000 feet in the
south.*

THE EUROPEAN ASH *(Fraxinus excelsior)*
*A native of Europe. It does not have the fall coloring of the
White Ash—the leaves tend to drop off when still green. The
bark is smooth and light gray on younger trees. The branches
are divided into pairs of four or eight and they are lance shaped
and tipped by a single leaflet which has sharp toothed margins
about three inches long. Greenish white or purplish flowers
which lack both petals and sepals appear prior to the leaves.
After fertilization the keys hang in clusters until the following
spring when they are carried off by the wind. Found in areas
where soil is damp; less common in sandy soils. Common in
parks and towns. This tree is popular in England and southern
Europe.*

THE FLOWERING ASH *(Fraxinus ornus)*
*Native to southern Europe and western Asia, it is now grown in
the Pacific Northwest. A sugary exudate called "manna" is ob-*

*tained from its sap which is used as a laxative. It attains a
height of twenty-five feet. The leaves are in pairs, pinnate, and
are about six to eight inches long. The leaflets grow in four pairs
and are one to two inches long, oval, and serrate. The flowers
are small, white, numerous, and about a sixth of an inch long.
The keys are about one inch long and one sixth of an inch wide.*

As an herb of the sun, ash is one of the trees that is
honored at the winter solstice. Its trunk and branches are
decorated with herbal offerings of holly, mistletoe and ivy and
gifts of cider and freshly baked cakes are placed at its base. Lit
candles are placed in the sacred four directions. Songs and
prayers are offered for the Trees of the World.

Ash is one of the sacred three—"Oak and Ash and
Thorn"—that are celebrated in British and Celtic songs and
legends. Ash was greatly revered by our ancestors for its healing powers and for its versatility as a building material. Tradition tells us that ash, like oak, is a tree that "Courts the flash"
and is best avoided during thunderstorms.

Native Americans believed ash was a tree that was sensitive to and in harmony with the Earth and her creatures. Ash
teaches us a mature understanding of emotions as it brings
soothing insights to problems.

People drawn to the ash cultivate peace of mind which
they share with those around them. They often become
teachers, counselors, history keepers, medicine people, and
herbalists. While ash people prefer to live in solitude, they will
make themselves available to others and may attract many
individuals to their circle.

Practical Uses

Elasticity is a major virtue of ash wood. Ash is a fast growing, strong wood that was used in the past to make spears,
bows, ax handles, ladders, carts, wagons, oars, carriages, walking sticks, hoops, and crates. It is second only to oak as a
building material. As a fuel, ash burns well with a hot flame
that produces very little smoke. Its bark has astringent properties and was used for tanning nets. Ash wood is also used to
make baskets. Like the people who resemble it, ash is strong,
yet pliable enough to bend.

The bark and leaves of the flowering ash are used to dye alum mordanted wool a yellow color. Wool mixed with copperas and ash will dye black.

Herbal Uses

The White Ash or European Ash are trees whose medicinal virtues are available year round. In spring and early summer, the young, tender tops and leaves are used to make a fasting tea that is both a diuretic and a laxative. (Herbal tradition recommends it as a weight loss aid.) The infusion also benefits jaundice, gout, and rheumatic conditions making it a classic spring tonic to burn off winter fat and to help clear out a body's system. In winter time, simply substitute the bark or the outer layer of the root when making the tea.

Ash leaves should be gathered in June, dried well, and then stored in airtight, opaque containers. These can be used to make a gentle laxative that is less harsh than one made with senna. One ounce of the leaves are infused for twenty minutes in a pint of just-boiled water and given in repeated doses over a twenty-four hour period.

Ash bark is known as a liver and spleen cleanser which means it can help strengthen the immune system. The bark has been used as an alternative to quinine to treat intermittent fevers, such as malaria, while the fruits or "keys" are used to allay gas pains. The keys can also be made into a substitute for capers when they are preserved in salt and vinegar. They will keep for one year if gathered when ripe.

The White Ash (Fraxinus Americana) is used homeopathically for uterine conditions, especially fibroids, uterine enlargement, and uterine tumors, and it is also useful to treat infantile eczema. The European Ash (Fraxinus Excelsior) is used homeopathically to treat gout and rheumatism. An infusion of the leaves is the recommended remedy.

Magical Uses

Ash is an herb of the sun whose element is Water. Poseidon, Woden, Thor, Mars, Gwydion, Neptune, and Uranus are all linked with ash.

Grieve's Herbal lists traditions associated with ash in the ancient lore of the British Isles. One involves the healing of a sick child by passing the child through a cleft in an ash sapling that has been split for this purpose. Another custom tells us to prick warts with new pins that have been first thrust into an ash. The pins are then stuck into the tree again and left there. The appropriate chant for the occasion is "ashen tree, ashen tree, pray buy these warts off of me."

Any place where oak and ash and thorn are seen together is a likely spot to find fairies. Some say the fairies were the "little people," the small dark race known as the Picts who were driven into the hills of Britain, Scotland, and Ireland by bigger folk. Perhaps the "little people," known to be wise in herb craft and the arts, knew the virtue of these trees.

A rich lore of magical tradition surrounds the ash. To the ancient Teutons, ash represented Yggdrasil, the "World Tree," a symbolic representation of the Creator's plan for the universe. The tree was said to spring from the primordial abyss and have three great roots—one for the future, one for the present, and one for the past.

Three large branches sprouted from the tree. The central branch supported the earth. Piercing it through its center, it issued from the mountain Asgard, home of the Gods. This central branch grew to overshadow the entire cosmos. Its leaves were the clouds, its flowers and fruit the stars. Another branch was guarded by the Norns or Fates, guardians of the past, present, and future, who sustained the tree by watering it daily. The water they drew came from a fountain in which two swans, the sun and the moon, resided. A wiseman, Mimir, the wisest of all men, lived near a fountain of the same name which was the source of all the waters on earth.

A clear honey-like dew called hunangsfall fell from the tree and provided food for bees. Four deer, symbolizing the four winds, darted in and out among the branches, nibbling the new shoots. An eagle perched on the highest branch, while a hawk, Veorfolnir, balanced on the eagle's head to give him advice. The eagle symbolized air, and the hawk, ether. Nidhoggr, the snake, was coiled at the foot of the tree and nibbled away at the roots. Serpents symbolized the fires at the center of the earth that threaten to overwhelm the world. A squirrel, Ratatösk (rain and snow), ran up and down the stem in an attempt to cause conflict between the snake and the eagle.

The horn, Giallr, which was to be blown by Heimdaller during the last great conflict, lay under the tree. Its sounds would call forth the twilight of the gods to bring an end to time, life, and the world.

Beyond the end, however, the world was to be reborn and the tree splendidly recreated. Two people named Lif (life) and Lifthrasir (desire of life), surviving the great conflict by hiding in the world ash, were to repopulate the earth. They would be nourished by the morning dew.

To the ancient Celts, ash symbolized the span of existence from past to present to future—Abred, Gwynedd, and Ceugant: Creation, Balance, and Destruction. These forces were said to be the sacred dimensions of every life's journey, death and destruction being nothing but a preparation for the next cycle of rebirth and creation. Thus the ash helps us to understand our place in the eternal cycles of the universe and how our private reality is part of the large Cosmic Dance.

Ash wood is one of the nine sacred woods deemed suitable for burning in ritual fires, and it has a special connection with the Yule celebration.

Ash is used in medicine bundles, sachets, and protective amulets. Ash wood, carved into crosses, offers protection from drowning which makes it appropriate to use in water and sea rituals.

Ash wands are suitable to use in healing magic. A druidic wand of ash from the first century A.D. with a spiral decoration carved on it was found in Anglesey, England. Witch's brooms are traditionally made from an ash staff with birch twigs and a willow binding completing the design. A staff of ash over the door guards the entrance from evil influences, and its green bark may be worn as a protective charm against sorcerers.

It is rumored that unicorns are fond of ash trees. To catch a glimpse of a unicorn, carry ash wood or leaves, or lie in a bed of ash and place its leaves on your chest.

Ash leaves placed under pillows induce prophetic dreams. Ash leaves scattered to the four directions will protect a house or an area. Carry a leaf to gain the love of the opposite sex.

Tradition holds that if one wants a newborn child to be a good singer, it is wise to bury its first nail parings under an ash. And remember—on no account sleep under an ash as it attracts lightning.

Weeping Willow

Willow
Watery Willow, Tree of the Moon

PEACHLEAF WILLOW (*Salix amygdaloides*)
This tree has one or more straight trunks, upright branches, and a spreading crown. It attains a height of sixty feet with a trunk diameter of two feet. The leaves are two to four and a half inches long and half to one and a quarter inches wide. The leaves are lanceolate, tapering to a point, saw-toothed, and slender. The bark is rough, dark brown, and furrowed. The flowers are catkins up to three inches long which appear in spring with the new leaves. The tree favors wet valley soils near streams and cottonwoods. Its range is from southeastern British Columbia to western Texas and New Mexico, and east to New York and northwestern Pennsylvania. It will grow in altitudes from 500 to 7000 feet.

THE WHITE WILLOW (*Salix alba*)
Native to Europe, North Africa and Western Asia, it was introduced to the U.S. in colonial times. The wood is used in England to make cricket bats. It has one to four trunks and an open, spreading crown. It attains a height of eighty feet and has a trunk diameter of two feet. Its leaves are two to four and a half inches long, three eighths to one and a quarter inches wide, lanceolate, finely saw-toothed, and they turn yellow in the fall. The bark is rough and gray with narrow furrows. The twigs droop slightly. The catkins appear in early spring and are up to two and a quarter inches long. It favors wet stream banks and low areas near cities.

THE WEEPING WILLOW (*Salix babylonica*)
Originally thought to be native to Babylon, it was also found in China. It probably came west along caravan routes. Easily identified by its short trunk and open crown of drooping branches, it attains a height of forty feet with a trunk diameter of two feet or more. The leaves are two and a half to five inches long, up to half an inch wide, and narrowly lanceolate with finely saw-toothed edges and long, pointed tips. The leaves are dark green above and whitish to gray beneath. The yellowish-green to

*brown twigs droop vertically. The catkins appear in the early
spring, are up to one inch long, and greenish. It is widely
planted in parks and cemeteries. It favors wet areas. Its range is
from southern Quebec and Ontario to Missouri and Georgia
and it has been introduced to the western states.*

THE GOAT WILLOW *(Salix caprea)*
*A European and north Asian native producing furry catkins in
the early spring that are about one and a half inches long. This
tree is cut back and fertilized to produce "pussy willows" for
flower shops. Favors damp wooded areas, scrub and hedges.
Common in northeastern United States on low, wet land and
riverbanks from Nova Scotia to Manitoba and south to
Delaware, West Virginia, Indiana, Illinois and northeastern
Montana.*

THE COYOTE WILLOW *(Salix exigua)*
*More shrub than tree, it grows in thickets to a height of twenty
feet with a trunk diameter of five inches. The leaves are very
narrow, long and pointed with scattered tiny teeth, hairless to
densely hairy, and yellowish-green to a grayish-green on both
sides. The bark is gray and smooth or slightly fissured. The twigs
are slender and upright. The catkins appear in spring, and are
about one to two and a half inches long with hairy yellow
scales. It prefers moist riverbanks, sandbars, and estuaries. Its
range is from Alaska to southern California, and east to
Quebec and Virginia. It will grow in altitudes to 8000 feet.*

THE CRACK WILLOW *(Salix fragilis)*
*A large tree with widely forking branches and very brittle twigs.
Introduced to North America in colonial times, it is native to
Europe and western Asia. The leaves are four to six inches long
and up to one and a half inches wide, lanceolate, coarsely saw-
toothed, and end in a point that turns to one side. They are
green above and whitish underneath. The bark is thick, rough,
and gray with deep, narrow ridges. The twigs are shiny, erect or
spreading with gummy buds. The catkins appear in spring and
are one to two and a half inches long, and yellow or greenish. It
prefers moist road sides, streams, and wet open areas. Its range
is from Newfoundland to Virginia to Kansas and South Dakota.*

THE BLACK WILLOW *(Salix nigra)*
*A prolific shade tree, honey plant, and constraint against soil
erosion and floods. It has one or more straight or leaning*

trunks, upright branches, and an irregular crown. It attains a height of up to one hundred feet and a trunk diameter of up to two and a half feet. The leaves are three to five inches long and three eighths to three quarters of an inch wide, narrow, lanceo-late, curved slightly to one side, and finely saw-toothed. They are paler green on the underside. The bark is deep brown to black, with deep scaly furrows and forking ridges. The twigs are slender and easily detached. It flowers in spring with yellow cat-kins that are one to three inches long. It favors wet stream banks and flood plains, and often grows near cottonwoods. Its range is from Maine to Florida, and southern Texas to Min-nesota. It is also found in northern Mexico and west to northern California.

THE PURPLE WILLOW *(Salix purpurea)*
Native to Europe and Asia, it was spread throughout the Americas by basket makers. A small tree of only six to ten feet with thin branches, green or reddish twigs, and a smooth and bitter bark. The leaves are oblanceolate, opposite or alternate, pointed, and finely toothed. The amount of salicin is judged by the bitterness of the bark and this species probably has more than any other. It favors wet meadowlands. Found in the east-ern and central United States on low ground, mostly along the Atlantic seaboard.

THE BASKET WILLOW *(Salix viminalis)*
A native of Eurasia, it was spread throughout the northeastern U.S. from Newfoundland to New England. An excellent tree for basket making and wicker work. It attains a height of twenty-five feet with a trunk diameter of six inches. The leaves are four to ten inches long and three eighths of an inch wide, narrow, lanceolate, without teeth, dull green on top, and white to gray beneath. The twigs are green, slender and flexible, and they be-come shiny with age. The catkins are up to one and a half in-ches long with a green-yellow hue and bloom before the leaves in spring. It favors wet areas, and is found near towns and set-tled areas.

The willow tree holds a special place in my heart as Willow is my "Craft" name. The name was given to me by a Lakota grandmother several years ago during a full moon ceremony in the woods. As a Druid initiate I often go by "Saille" which is Irish (Gaelic) for willow. "Sally" rods were used for thatching on traditional Celtic homes. To native Americans the willow is a feminine tree that carries the essence of the healing touch. It should be noted that the "Weeping Willow" is a native of China and that it does not necessarily figure into Native American or Celtic tradition.

Practical Uses

Colonists to the Americas valued the willow as a shade tree and for its wood that was good for fence posts and fuel.

The Peachleaf Willow, a plains species, is used to protect riverbanks from erosion. One of the great blessings of the willow is its water loving nature. If a garden or field tends to flood, try introducing a graceful willow tree. It will dry the soil while adding subtle beauty to the landscape.

The Native Americans use the twigs and bark of the Coyote Willow for baskets. The leaves are now used as fodder for livestock. The Crack Willow was used to make charcoal for gunpowder. The Basket Willow is the willow most often used for wicker work and baskets.

The Black Willow is the largest willow and its wood has been used for furniture, millwork, cabinets, doors, barrels, boxes, toys, and pulp. It was prized by the American colonists as a honey tree.

In addition to these properties, willow is also valued in England as material for making cricket bats.

Herbal Uses

The graceful, water-loving willow has been used for years as a pain-relieving agent. Only recently has it been usurped from its healing role by a synthetic substitute called aspirin. Willow bark contains a glucoside called salicin that forms salicylous acid in the body which is the "active ingredient" in aspirin.

Willow bark is useful to alleviate pain and lower fevers although it is wise to remember that fevers are Mother Nature's way of "cooking the germs" and unless a really high fever persists we are generally better off letting a fever run its course. Invading pathogens have a very narrow margin of temperature in which they can survive and by allowing the body to activate its defenses we are strengthening our immune systems while destroying the microbes.

Willow has been known as an astringent tonic since ancient times and was recognized as a remedy for intermittent fevers by western Europeans in 1763. It was not as valued as quinine (chinchona), however, and was mostly used to heal a high fever in conjunction with diarrhea.

Versatile willow bark is used to treat rheumatic conditions, gout, heartburn, and, due to its astringency, it helps to stop internal bleeding. It is useful as a diuretic, as a gargle for sore throats and gums, and it makes a good external wash for sores, skin problems, wounds, and burns.

The White Willow is most commonly used as an herbal remedy. The Purple Willow has the same general properties as the White Willow and is even more effective in lowering fevers. The Black Willow also has these virtues, plus an infusion of its bark and catkins is a sexual sedative. The Sallow or Goat Willow eases indigestion, whooping cough and catarrh, and is used as an antiseptic to disinfect bandages.

Culpeper recommends using the sap of the flowering tree to benefit the eyes. Use it as a wash or drink it. Taken orally, it clears the skin and face of blemishes. A decoction of the leaves or bark, simmered lightly, is used to treat dandruff.

Willow can be used to prevent recurring fevers or as a digestive tonic, especially for dyspepsia related to a debility of the digestive organs.

Black Willow bark is used to treat gonorrhoea, to relieve ovarian pain, and to curb nocturnal emissions. The White Willow bark has been used to treat chronic diarrhea and dysentery. Willow bark tea is combined with borax to make a deodorizing washing aid.

Willow bark is collected in the spring. To make the tea, soak one to three teaspoons of the bark in one cup of cold water for two to five hours, then simmer lightly for twenty minutes. The dose is one cup per day taken in teaspoon quantities. Alternatively, soak one tablespoon of the bark in cold water for eight to ten hours and strain. One to two teaspoons of powdered bark can be used three times per day in tea or capsules.

A poultice for gangrene and ulcers is made by simmering the powdered bark in cream.

Dr. Bach recommends the willow flower essence as the remedy for bitterness and resentment. People who blame others for their problems would benefit from the willow flower essence. Likewise, people who feel they have been treated unfairly by fate, who alienate others, and who fail to see themselves as the source of their own misfortunes, may also be helped by this essence. In the positive state, such people exhibit optimism and faith, and they recognize their responsibility for creating their destiny through their thoughts and deeds.

As with all flower essences, the willow remedy acts on the subtle, etheric body to remove the negative emotional states that are often the origin of disease.

A tincture of fresh Black Willow bark (Salix Nigra) is used in homeopathy for hysteria and nervous conditions associated with the genital organs. Nymphomania, spermatorrhoea, satyriasis, erotomania, and lascivious dreams are treated with this herb, especially when accompanied by ovarian or testicular pain.

Magical Uses

Willow, associated with the element of Water, is an herb of the moon, and is sacred to Artemis, Ceres, Hecate, Persephone, Hera, Mercury, Belili, Circe, and Belenos. Willow is also associated with the death aspect of the triple Moon Goddess. The lovely willow has qualities of femininity and love, thereby aiding in love divination, protection, and healing. The tree seems to have a feminine essence that speaks of friendship, love, and joy. The branches sweep away tears and bring peace.

The lesson of the willow is her flexible nature. She speaks of loyalty and the ability to listen with gentle kindness. She illuminates the value of soft-spoken words combined with a joyful enthusiasm about life.

The Native Americans see the willow as a tree of gentle humility, charm, and graceful elegance. The Seneca call it the "whispering one."

In the Lakota tradition, tobacco and willow are smoked together in the sacred pipe because the willow's energy helps the tobacco ascend to the heavens.

Willow strengthens that part of us that acts on our dreams. Intuition, knowledge, and gentle nurturing are found in the willow's quiet touch. As an herb of the moon, willow will elucidate the feminine qualities of both men and women.

Willow is generally found near sources of water or in swampy areas. Ancient burial mounds in the British Isles that are near water were often lined with willows, perhaps to help keep them from being damaged by moisture. Funerary flints were cut in a willow leaf shape.

Willow leaves are used in herbal mixtures designed to attract love, and its wood is used to make wands for moon magic. Willow is often used by dowsers to locate underground water, earth energies, and buried objects.

To determine if you will be married in the new year, throw a shoe into a willow on New Year's Eve. If the shoe sticks you will be married within twelve months. Willow wood carried or placed in the home guards against evil. A willow tree growing near a home will provide protection.

Willow leaves, bark, and wood add energy to healing magic. Willow bark and sandalwood *Santalum album* mixed and burned together during the waning moon may conjure spirits. Carrying a piece of willow wood helps to overcome the fear of death.

The enchantress Circe was reputed to have lived in a thick willow grove on the island of Aenea. The Ainee of Japan see the willow as a sacred tree and venerate the mistletoe that grows upon it. Orpheus was said to receive the gift of eloquence after touching the willows in Persephone's grove.

The early Irish tell the tale of King Maon, also called Labra the Mariner, who had the ears of a horse. Whenever he needed his hair cut, he would execute the hairdresser so as to keep his ears a secret. One time a poor widow's son was chosen to do the job and through his mother's entreaties and a vow to keep silent he was spared. Finding it hard to keep the secret to himself, he sought the advice of a druid who told him to whisper it to a willow tree.

Soon after, a harper named Craftiny was searching for wood to make a new harp and he cut down the willow. When the harp was built he played on it for the king. To everyone's amazement the harp cried out: "Labra the Mariner has two horses ears." After that the king never put another haircutter to death.

If you wish to make manifest something in your life, tie a knot on a willow branch as you visualize your intention. When you receive what you asked for, untie the knot and use it again.

An old Celtic custom consists of tying prayer-cloths to trees that are near sacred fountains or wells. Water was seen as the entrance to the Otherworld in Celtic thought and the cloths were left tied to a nearby tree to send the prayers into the wind.

Trees purify the air;
they also purify the mind...
if you want to save your world,
you must save the trees.
— The Trees of Endor

What does he plant who plants a tree?
He plants a friend of sun and sky;
He plants the flag of breezes free;
The shaft of beauty, towering high;
He plants a home to heaven anigh
For song and mother-croon of bird
In hushed and happy twilight heard—
The treble of heaven's harmony—
These things he plants who plants a tree.

What does he plant who plants a tree?
He plants cool shade and tender rain,
And seed and bud of days to be,
And years that fade and flush again;
He plants the glory of the plain;
He plants the forest's heritage;
The harvest of a coming age;
The joy that unborn eyes shall see—
These things he plants who plants a tree.

What does he plant who plants a tree?
He plants, in sap and leaf and wood,
In love of home and loyalty
And far-cast thought of civic good—
His blessing on the neighborhood
Who in the hollow of His hand
Holds all the growth of all our land—
A nation's growth from sea to sea
Stirs in his heart who plants a tree.
— Henry C. Bunner

American Holly

Holly

Holly makes a Haven for Spirits of the Wood

AMERICAN HOLLY *(Ilex opaca)*
A narrow, rounded, evergreen tree with a closely packed crown
of spiny leaves, white flowers and red berries. It can grow to
seventy feet with a trunk diameter of two feet. The leaves spread
in two rows and are up to four inches long and one and a half
inches wide. They are thick, stiff, and elliptical, with spiny
points, dull green above and yellower beneath. The bark can be
smooth or rough and bumpy. It is generally light gray.
The twigs are grey or brown and hairy when immature.
The flowers, are a quarter inch wide and are white with four
petals and found in clumps at the bases of new leaves and
twigs. The male and female flowers appear on separate trees in
the spring. The berries are a quarter to three eighths inch in
diameter and mature in autumn. The tree likes moist or wet
soil in mixed hardwood forests. It grows from Massachusetts to
Florida and from Texas to Missouri up to 4000 feet.

ENGLISH HOLLY *(Ilex aquifolium)*
A southern European, north African, and west Asian evergreen.
A male plant is required to pollinate the female so that it can
produce berries. It has a conical crown, spreading branches,
and bright shiny red berries. It grows to a height of fifty feet with
a trunk diameter of one and a half feet. The leaves are up to
two and three quarter inches long, elliptical with spiny points,
wavy edged, blunt based, and stiff. They are shiny, dark green
above and pale beneath. The bark is gray and nearly smooth.
The twigs are purple or green, angled, and they may have stout
hairs. The flowers are a quarter of an inch wide, white, have
four petals, with male and female blossoms on separate trees,
and they bloom in late spring. The berries are small in diameter,
shiny red, ripen in autumn, and they remain attached all winter.
It favors moist soils in humid regions, especially the American
east coast to southern New England, and the Pacific coast.

DAHOON HOLLY *(Ilex cassine)*
An evergreen native to the southeastern United States. A small

*tree with a rounded crown and dense clusters of fruit. It grows
to thirty feet with a trunk diameter of one foot. The leaves are
oblong or ovate, without teeth or spines, up to three and a half
inches long and up to one and a quarter inches wide, shiny
dark green above, and lighter beneath. They are hairy when
young. The bark is dark gray and varies from smooth to rough.
The twigs are covered with silky hairs. The flowers are small
and white, with four rounded petals, and they grow at the base
of the new spring leaves. The berries are a quarter of an inch in
diameter, shiny red, yellow, or orange. They mature in autumn
and remain attached in winter. It favors swampy, sandy or
brackish soil. Its range is from southern Florida to southeastern
North Carolina and southern Louisiana. It grows in altitudes to
200 feet.*

"Christmastide comes in like a bride, with Holly and Ivy
clad." This charming old verse comes from Grieve's Herbal.
To the ancients, holly was symbolic of male energy. Twining
ivy was seen as the female essence. Thus crowns of ivy and
holly were bestowed upon newlywed couples. It is said that the
druids decorated their homes with holly as a sign to the Woodland Spirits that they would find a safe refuge there from the
storms of winter.

In the ancient Roman feast of Saturnalia, which took place
about a week before Christmas at the time of the winter
solstice, gifts decorated with bits of holly were given. A classic
tree for Christmas decorations, it provides winter food for
birds and wild animals. It is interesting to reflect on how much
of our ancient heritage is still with us in our seasonal celebrations of today.

 ## Practical Uses

Holly berries are attractive as decorations, but internal use
should be avoided by humans. Culpeper informs us that they
were used in cases of colic, but that they can be drastic purgatives. Wild birds, however, eat them with great relish and
suffer no ill effects. The holly leaves provide winter fodder for
deer, and the young stems have been dried and used as cow
fodder. A stick of holly placed in a rabbit hutch acts as a tonic
and appetite stimulant.

Holly has a very fine white wood that in the past was used for inlays and fine ornamental carving. Its even grain makes it valuable for detailed woodwork. Walking sticks and riding crops were often made of this wood.

The holly tree is considered masculine and it provided wood for the ancient Celts to make spear shafts.

Herbal Uses

English Holly is a traditional herbal of great repute. Holly leaves are used either fresh or dry. They are collected in May or June at midday during dry weather. The infusion is given for catarrh, pleurisy, smallpox, intermittent fevers, and rheumatism. Their action is slightly diuretic to the kidneys, and dilating to the arteries. The infusion produces sweating, and thus it benefits fevers and rheumatism.

In the Black Forest of Germany, holly leaves were used as a substitute for tea. Holly berries are emetic and purgative, and internal use should probably be avoided by the inexperienced lay person. They can be dried and powdered and then used externally to stop bleeding. Culpeper recommends external fomentations of the bark and leaves for broken bones and dislocated joints.

For coughs, colds, and the flu, infuse half an ounce of the chopped leaves in one pint of just boiled water. Let them steep for about twenty minutes, then strain and drink the fluid in one ounce doses.

As a flower essence, holly is the remedy for anger, envy, jealousy, and suspicion. It is the antidote for hatred. In the words of Dr. Bach: "holly protects us from everything that is not Universal Love." He suggested using holly when no other remedy was apparent, seeing lack of love as the ultimate foundation of any negative emotional state.

People who need holly are active, intense individuals who are filled with insecurities, aggressions, suspicion, envy, and anger. On the positive side, they are beings of unconditional love, who give to the world without expecting anything in return. These people continue to be loving, tolerant, and happy even after suffering great losses, and they enjoy seeing others succeed in life.

The English Holly (Ilex Aquifolium) is used homeopathically for intermittent fevers, eye symptoms, and pain in the spleen.

Magical Uses

Holly, a tree of Saturn and Mars, and of the element Fire, is sacred to Lugh, the Celtic God of Light, and to Habondia, Goddess of Plenty. It is one of the Nine Sacred Woods used in ritual fires. (The nine are: oak, pine, holly, hazel, juniper, cedar, poplar, apple, and ash.) A seventh century portion of the ancient Irish law, Crith Gablach, lists the seven noble sacred trees of the grove as birch, alder, willow, oak, holly, hazel, and apple.

Holly is a tree of protection often used as an anti-lightning charm, and it is planted around the house as a general safeguard. Holly is said to guard against poison, evil spirits, and evil sorcerers, and it will repel dangerous wild animals. An infusion of holly can be sprinkled on newborn babies as a protective charm.

Gather nine holly leaves in complete silence on a Friday after midnight. Place them on a white cloth. Using nine knots to bind the cloth, place it under your pillow to make your dreams come true.

For the ancient Celts, the year was divided into halves ruled by the Summer Lord and the Winter Lord, respectively. The Green Knight, an immortal giant armed with a holly club, battles with the hero Cuchulain as they attempt to behead each other on alternate New Years—midsummer and midwinter.

This tradition is a version of the yearly struggle between the Lord of Winter and the Lord of Summer. At the fall equinox the Green Man or Lord of Summer yields to the Horned God, or Lord of Winter. The Lord of Summer rules when the warm earth is covered with leaves, flowers, grasses, and grain. The Winter Lord governs in the cold of the year when only meat is available as food. At the spring equinox, the Horned God of the hunt must once again give way to the Green Man. Traditional societies often enacted this ancient drama in the form of a ritual combat.

Holly is a warrior tree whose thorns defend him in the dark cold of winter. A spear of the holly gives focus and direction

to spiritual struggles. It will sharpen your wits and give you the
courage to succeed in your quest.

In the woods is perpetual youth.
Within these plantations of God a
decorum and sanctity reign,
a perennial festival is dressed,
and a guest sees not
how he should tire of them
in a thousand years.
— Ralph Waldo Emerson

Black Hawthorn

Hawthorn

Hawthorn, the May Day Flower

ENGLISH HAWTHORN *(Crataegus oxyacantha)*
A popular European and north African tree known as the "May Tree" in English literature. It attains a height of thirty feet and lives to a great age. Flowers may be white, pink, or deep red, five eighths of an inch in diameter, and they bloom in May. The fruits are bright red and resemble a miniature apple and the foliage does not turn color in the fall. The leaves alternate with thorns. It thrives in poor soils that can be either acid or alkaline. It is a member of the rose family. A favorite in American gardens.

The Latin name for hawthorn is *Crataegus oxyacantha*, which comes to us from the Greek kratos (hardness), oxus (sharp), and akantha (a thorn). Haw is an ancient word for hedge, and in Germany and the British Isles this tree was commonly used to separate fields.

Practical Uses

The wood of hawthorn is fine grained and suitable for use in inlays and delicate carvings. The rootwood is finer still and is suitable for making boxes and combs.

Of all trees, hawthorn creates the hottest wood fire. In the past it was more highly prized than oak for heating ovens and hawthorn charcoal can produce a fire that would melt pig iron.

Herbal Uses

The hawthorn berry is one of the finest cardiac tonics available. It seems to benefit almost all heart related conditions. It normalizes blood pressure (but can cause low blood pressure if used over a long time). Functional heart problems such as murmurs, leaky valves, inflammation of heart muscles, arteriosclerosis, fatty degeneration of vessels, dropsy of cardiac origin, and aortic diseases of all kinds will benefit from using hawthorn berries. Of course when undertaking the management or cure of a complex condition such as heart disease, it is wise to add additional remedies such as a change in diet, exercise, and sleep patterns. A health professional should be consulted.

Crataegus, a homeopathic remedy made from the hawthorn berry, is used primarily as a heart tonic. Myocanditis, irregularity of heart beat, oedema, and high arterial tension, chronic heart disease with weakness, feeble heart action, arteriosclerosis, painful pressure on the left side of the chest, and heart failure will all be benefited. It is suitable for irritable patients with cardiac symptoms, and those with apprehension, insomnia, and despondency. It can also be used for diabetes in young children.

Use of the berries may help in the prevention of future problems. They help tone the heart, and will improve resistance in the face of infections such as strep, rheumatic fever, and tonsillitis, all of which have been known to injure the heart.

It is wise not to use hawthorn alone as it is a powerful herb. Mix it with borage, motherwort, cayenne, garlic, and dandelion flowers for a long term heart program. You will probably want to have these herbs milled and placed in capsules, or you can ingest the garlic and cayenne in capsule form with your meals.

For short term use (two to three weeks), steep one teaspoon of the flowers in half a cup of water for twenty minutes. Drink up to one and a half cups per day taken in teaspoonful doses. You may also steep one teaspoon of the crushed fruit (berries) in half a cup of water for twenty minutes and drink one and a half cups a day in teaspoonful doses. If cold water is preferable, place one teaspoon of the crushed fruit in half a cup and let it stand for seven to eight hours. Boil briefly and strain. The dose is one and a half cups per day in repeated small quantities.

Hawthorn leaves can substitute for Oriental green tea, and the seeds can be roasted and used in a manner similar to coffee. For those attempting to break the tobacco habit, the young leaves can be smoked in a nicotine-free cigarette. Yarrow, mint, coltsfoot, and mullein can be added for variety, and to help heal the throat.

French homeopaths have developed a series of homeo-pathic remedies called "drainage remedies" because they stimulate the organs of excretion and help to clean glands and tissues. In this system a low potency (2x) of Hawthorn bud tincture is used to increase myocardial tone, especially in the left side of the heart. The dose is fifty drops, once a day, in water.

Hawthorn Jam

(Gather the fruits after the first frost.)
3 qts. berries
5 cups honey
1 cup water
1 box Sure-Jell
1/2 lemon, sliced

Simmer the berries and lemon until they are soft. Squeeze out the juice, add the Sure-Jell, and mix. Bring to a quick boil over high heat. Add honey and boil for one minute. Remove from heat and pour into glasses, leaving half the jar empty. Cover with paraffin and seal.

May Brandy

Fill a jar with hawthorn flowers (be sure not to include the stems). Cover with whiskey or brandy and allow to sit for two to three months. Strain and rebottle.

Hawthorn Cocktail

1 bottle white wine
sprig of lemon thyme
1/2 bottle red wine
two sprigs of borage
1 orange, sliced
a handful of hawthorn flowers

Pour the wine into a bowl. Add orange slices, herbs, and flowers. Cover with a cloth and let stand for a day and a half. Strain and shake with ice in a cocktail shaker. Decorate glasses with borage flowers.

Magical Uses

Hawthorn bears a special relationship to May Day, the ancient cross quarter day known to the ancients as Beltane, which is celebrated in honor of the sun god Belenos. The true date for this festival was reckoned as the first morning that the hawthorn blossoms opened. It is one of the sacred three of British and Celtic antiquity: "Oak, and Ash, and Thorn." When these trees grow together it is said to be a favorite haunt of the fairies. To this day, in Ireland, it is considered a woeful thing to cut down a "Fairy Tree."

In ancient Greece and Rome, hawthorn was employed in fertility celebrations and rituals. It was associated with marriage and babies, and was sacred to Hymen, the God of marriage. Bridal attendants wore its blossoms, and brides carried whole branches. Torches used in wedding processions were made of hawthorn. Interestingly, its leaves were placed under the bed or around the bedroom as an aid for preserving chastity. Hawthorn leaves were placed in the cradle as a protective charm after the birth of a child.

Medieval European tradition held that the hawthorn was a favorite tree of witches, and that they could transform themselves into a hawthorn tree at will. When you consider the value of hawthorn as a healing agent, there is probably some truth to that assertion. Many witches were known to be practitioners of "green magic," or the healing arts, and they could have been seen near the trees when gathering their useful gifts.

Hawthorn is a tree of Mars, and is of the Fire element. It is sacred to Cardea, Flora, Hymen, and Thor, and bestows powers of fertility, chastity, fishing magic, and joyful celebration. At Beltane (May Day), it is customary to decorate the top of a May pole with its boughs. Magical rites of all kinds can be performed under a "thorn."

The chaste hawthorn will help keep you on track when a period of waiting and inner silence is called for. She will focus your attention until the moment when renewed activity and fertile progress arrives.

Carry a piece of "thorn" in a pouch to bring good luck when fishing. Use it as an amulet to ward off depression and restore happiness.

Hang hawthorn from a high point of a building to protect it from lightning.

Always trim hawthorn hedges from east to west, in a sunwise direction. Never cut a blooming tree (it angers the Fairies).

Elaborate legends surround the hawthorn. One is the story of the "Glastonbury Thorn" that used to grow on the island of Avalon in Somerset, England. The reverence in which this tree was held was probably a remnant of the ancient respect given it in pre-Christian times. This regard was carried into the middle ages.

The legend of the Glastonbury Thorn speaks of Joseph of Arimathea who brought a staff of hawthorn from Palestine when he travelled to England to proselytize. At that time, Avalon was by the sea, and when Joseph landed at Glastonbury he thrust his staff into the ground where it miraculously rooted and flowered. He decided to build a church on the site. Eventually, the abbey of Glastonbury was built there and the famous tree was venerated by pilgrims until 1750 when it's stump was replaced by a stone marker.

To the ancient Teutons, hawthorn was sacred to Thor, the storm God. They made funeral pyres of the wood believing that the souls of the dead would escape via the burning thorns and thus ascend to the sky. The sacred hawthorn fire, to these people, was a mirror of the celestial fire-lightning.

A Scottish legend tells of two boys who were plowing a field in which an ancient hawthorn was growing. One of the boys drew a circle around the "Fairy tree" to protect it from the plow. Instantly, a table covered with delicious food appeared in the circle. The lad who had drawn the circle ate the food, but the other refused. He who ate the fairy offerings became wise ever after.

In ancient Ireland, the destruction of a hawthorn tree was considered a dangerous thing. Such action could result in the death of one's cattle or children, and the loss of all well being.

Holy thorns grew near sacred wells where pilgrims would tear off bits of their clothing and hang them on the trees (a practice that continues to this day). These bits of clothing might be left as an offering after a cure or they might serve as prayer flags wafting their prayers for health and healing to the breezes. It was hoped that the prayers would go out to the Gods via the medium of the tree and the wind. An interesting side light is that solitary hawthorn trees growing on hills or near sacred wells were considered to be markers that showed an entrance to the world of faery. The prayers were thus being offered to the fairies as well.

American Filbert

Hazel

Hazel, Tree of Immortal Wisdom

EUROPEAN HAZEL *(Corylus avellana)*
A large variety grown chiefly for its nuts and found in Oregon and Washington state. Its branches are smooth, pliable, and tough. The leaves are large and round with indented edges. The male flowers are yellow, drooping catkins. It grows to fifteen feet.

AMERICAN FILBERT *(Corylus americana)*
An American native of the family Cupuliferae with white and generally hard wood. It has alternate leaves that are pinnately veined, and are two to five inches long. The nuts are small and rounded, half an inch wide, and two to four grow in a cluster. It grows to nine feet and is found from Nova Scotia and Newfoundland to northern Pennsylvania, and from British Columbia to New Mexico and across the central plains.

BEAKED FILBERT *(Corylus cornuta)*
Native to Quebec, Saskatchewan, Georgia, and Missouri. The nuts are about half an inch wide. It attains a height of six feet.

CALIFORNIA FILBERT *(Corylus rostrata, var. californica)*
Is a tree with white, hard wood, alternate leaves, pinnately veined, with sterile flowers in its catkins and fertile flowers furnished with a scaly cup or bur to form a receptacle for the nuts. Of the family Cupuliferae, it grows from British Columbia to central California and flowers in February or March.

Hazel is grown as an ornamental and a food tree. Most of the species provide food for wild animals, but the European Hazel is used in the commercial production of filberts. This tree also provides excellent cover for wildlife.

Practical Uses

The California Filbert is used for erosion control, animal and human food, casket splints, and is an ingredient in medicinal treatments.

The nuts are harvested by hand as soon as the edges of the husks begin to brown. Gathering must be accomplished quickly or much will be lost to squirrels and other wildlife. Hazelnuts can be roasted, candied, or ground into flour.

Herbal Uses

French schools of homeopathy favor hazel as a "drainage remedy." Such a remedy is generally given as an "intercurrent," at times when the exact "Similimum" or constitutional remedy has not yet been found or when the constitutional remedy seems to have stopped working. The buds of Corylus Avellana are prepared in a low (2x) potency which restores elasticity to lung tissue. Emphysema, plumonarry fibrosis and some liver conditions are benefitted by this remedy. The dose is fifty drops of tincture, once a day, in water.

Hazelnuts are a food source that is rich in phosphorus, magnesium, potassium, copper, protein, and unsaturated fatty acids. Culpeper recommends powdering the nuts and mixing them with mead or honeyed water to help a chronic cough. Pepper can be added to the mixture to draw mucous from the sinus passages.

Hazelnut Cookies
> *2 cups ground hazelnuts*
> *1 tablespoon grated lemon peel*
> *1/2 cup honey*
> *1 egg, beaten*
> *1/4 cup flour*
> *1 tablespoon lemon juice*

Blend the honey and ground nuts into a paste. Mix in the flour and the lemon peel. Blend the lemon juice with the beaten egg and add this mixture to the nut batter. Drop by tablespoonfuls onto a greased cookie sheet. Bake at 350 degrees for twenty minutes.

Hazelnut Soup
> *1 cup vegetable or chicken stock*
> *2 tablespoons oil*
> *1 teaspoon thyme*

1 cup milk
1 teaspoon parsley
1 cup ground nuts
1 teaspoon tarragon
1 chopped onion

Saute the onions in oil. Add all other ingredients and simmer gently for fifteen minutes.

Magical Uses

The hazel tree, associated with the element Air, is an herb of the sun, and is sacred to Mercury, Thor, Artemis, and Diana. Hazel trees bestow fertility, protection, and wisdom.

The hazelnut is sweet and compact, symbolizing the concentrated wisdom and the life sustaining energies of the sun.

The hazel tree was venerated by the ancient Celts for having a special association with sacred springs and wells. To the Celts, water was seen as the entrance to the Otherworld and offerings could be made to the Gods by dropping hazelnuts into lakes and wells.

Connla's Well is described in the Dindsenchas, an early Irish poem. It was located near Tipperary, under the Nine Hazels of Poetry that gave their flowers (beauty) and fruit (wisdom) simultaneously. Sacred salmon swimming in the well swallowed the nuts as they fell into the water and developed one bright spot on their skin for every nut they consumed. These nuts were said to give birth to all the knowledge of art and science.

The hazel can also be a symbol of wisdom put to foul uses as in the Fenian legend of the Ancient Dripping Hazel, which was barren, dripped poison, and was home to vultures and ravens. When the hero Fionn used its wood for a battle shield, it gave off fumes that killed thousands.

Hazel was one of the "Seven Chieftain Trees" protected by the ancient Brehon Law of Ireland. The felling of such a tree was punishable by a fine of one cow. A commentator on the Brehon Law explains why these seven trees are venerated. Oak is noble due to its beauty and size, and because of the acorns which are used for pig fodder. Hazel is noble because of its wattles and nuts; apple for its valuable bark (used for tanning) and its fruit; yew for its timber which is used for bows, breast plates, and household implements; holly for its wood which is used to make the shafts of chariots; ash for its wood which used in the shafts of weapons, the royal throne, and spears; and pine for its wood used in flooring and casks. (And, as we have seen, parts of these trees can make valuable medicines.)

The forked branches of hazel were traditionally used to search for hidden objects, water, and persons guilty of robbery and murder. In the same way that hazel twigs are used to divine new wells and water sources, the wood of hazel can help to divine the pure source of poetry and wisdom. Use its powers to enhance your intuitive knowledge and your creative impulses.

Bind two hazel twigs into an equal armed cross by winding red thread or yarn around them. This will bring good fortune.

The best time to gather hazel for magical work is after sundown on Samhain (Hallowe'en). Hazel twigs can be used to draw a circle on the ground that will make a "ring-pass-not" for psychic protection, or to delineate sacred spaces. Its wood is also said to be an anti-lightning charm.

Wear a hazel crown to strengthen wish manifestation. Legend says that this crown will impart invisibility to the wearer.

An old tradition holds that three pieces of hazel wood driven into the walls of a house will protect it from fire.

In England, the hazelnut was used for love divination on Samhain (Hallowe'en) which is also known as "nutcrack night." To accomplish this you must assign the name of your sweetheart to a hazelnut. Place it in the fire and see if it leaps out of the flame or burns brightly. You will then know if your love is destined to be a great passion or if it will ultimately fail. In the words of the poet Thomas Gray:

> *Two hazelnuts I threw into the flame*
> *And to each nut I gave a sweetheart's name*
> *This, with the loudest bounce me sore amazed.*
> *That, with a flame of brightest color blazed.*
> *As blazed the nut, so may thy passion grow,*
> *For 'twas thy nut that did so brightly glow.*

O beech, unbind your yellow leaf, for deep
The honeyed time lies sleeping, and lead shade
Seals up the eyelids of its golden sleep.
Long are your flutes, chimes, little bells at rest,
And here is only the cold scream of the fox,
Only the hunter following on the hound,
And your quaint-plumaged,
The bird that your green happy boughs lapped round,
Bends south its soft bright breast.

Before the winter and the terror break,
Scatter the leaf that broadened with the rose,
Not for a tempest, but a sigh to take.
Four nights to exorcise the thing that stood,
Bound by these frail which dangle at your branch,
They ran a frosty dagger to its heart,
And it, wan substance,
No more remembered it might cry, or start,
Or stain a point with blood.

— Leonie Adams

Paper Birch

Birch
Shining Birch, the Lady of the Woods

YELLOW BIRCH *(Betula alleghaniensis = Betula lutea)*
A native of damp woods from Newfoundland to Georgia. It has a broad, rounded crown with drooping branches. It grows to a height of one hundred feet with a trunk diameter of two and a half feet. The leaves are three to five inches long and one and a half inches wide, elliptical, short-pointed, rounded at the base, and doubly saw-toothed with nine to eleven veins on each side. They are darker green above, and yellow in autumn. The fragrance of wintergreen emanates from its crushed leaves and twigs. The bark is shiny yellow to silver gray with papery, curly strips, becoming brownish red and scaly with age. The flowers bloom in spring. The male flowers are yellow with two stamens and grow as long drooping catkins near twig tips. The female flowers are greenish, short, and on the back of the tip of the same twig as the one upon which the male flowers grow. The cones are three quarters of an inch to one and a quarter inches long, oblong, hairy, brown, and upright in autumn. It favors moist uplands and ravines and is found with conifers and hardwoods. Its range is from southeastern Manitoba to southern Newfoundland, and northeastern Georgia to northeastern Iowa. It grows to altitudes of 2500 feet in the north and 3000 to 6000 feet in the south.

SWEET BIRCH OR BLACK BIRCH *(Betula lenta)*
It is native to the eastern United States. Its shape is pyramidal when young, and it gets more rounded with maturity. It grows to eighty feet and with a trunk diameter of up to two and a half feet. The leaves are up to five inches long, up to three inches wide, elliptical, long-pointed and notched at the base, sharply and double-toothed, with nine to eleven veins on each side. They are lighter green beneath and bright yellow in the fall. It has aromatic twigs and leaves when crushed. It produces tiny flowers in the early spring. The male flowers are yellowish with two stamens and grow in long drooping catkins near twig tips. The female flowers are greenish and grow in short upright cat-

kins on the same twig. The cones are three quarters of an inch to one and a half inches long, oblong, brown, upright, and they mature in autumn. The bark is shiny and dark, resembling cherry. The trees flourish in rugged terrain from southern Maine to northern Alabama and Ohio. They are also found in southern Quebec and southeastern Ontario. They grow at sea level in the north and to altitudes of 2000 to 6000 feet in the south.

CANOE BIRCH *(Betula papyrifea)*
A common ornamental native to central northeastern North America. It grows to ninety feet. It has a narrow open crown with drooping and horizontal branches. It can have a trunk diameter of up to two feet. The leaves are two to four inches long, up to two inches wide, ovate, long, pointed, doubly sawtoothed, with five to nine veins on each side. They are paler green beneath and golden-yellow in autumn. The bark is white, smooth and thin, separating into papery strips, covering and an orange inner bark that becomes brown upon exposure to air. It produces tiny flowers in early spring. The male are yellowish with two stamens, and grow in long drooping catkins at twig tips. The female are greenish, short, upright, and grow on the back of same twig tip. The cones are up to two inches long, narrow, cylindrical, brown, and they mature in autumn. It favors moist and disturbed soils from northwestern Alaska to Labrador, New York to Oregon, and Colorado to western North Carolina. They grow in altitudes to 4000 feet.

EUROPEAN WHITE BIRCH *(Betula alba)*
It has an open pyramidal crown with drooping branches. A native of Europe and Asia Minor. It grows to a height of fifty feet with a trunk diameter of one foot. The leaves are one and a quarter to two and three quarter inches long, up to one and a half inches wide, doubly saw-toothed with six to nine veins on each side, pale underneath, and yellow in the fall. The bark is white, smooth, flaky, and peels off in papery strips. The twigs are slender and drooping. The flowers are tiny and appear in early spring. The male are yellow with two stamens, and grow in long drooping catkins near twig tips. The female are greenish, short, and upright on back of same twig. The cones are three quarters to one and a quarter inches long, cylindrical, and they mature in the fall. It favors moist lawns, thickets and forest areas. Found in North America from Newfoundland west to British Columbia and south to the northeastern United States.

The beautiful, White Birches with their slender, pale trunks seem to embody an ideal of graceful femininity. A stand of White Birches against a clear blue sky expresses a positive light-filled grace that is unequaled in the kingdom of trees.

The word birch may be derived from the ancient Sanskrit bharg meaning shining, or possibly from bhurga which is "a tree whose bark is good to write upon." The word may come to us from the Anglo-Saxon beorgan, "to protect or shelter."

Less poetically, it may be derived from the Latin batuere, "to strike." A bundle of birch rods surrounding an axe was the ancient symbol of the Roman empire's power to punish by flogging (the birch rods), or death (the axe).

Practical Uses

The wood of the birch is soft and light. It is used for humbler objects of the household and trade such as furniture, wooden spoons, tool handles, brooms, bobbins, and barrel staves. It's twigs are used for thatching and wattles on traditional homes in England, Scotland, France, Ireland, Holland, Denmark, etc. Birch charcoal is used in gun powder.

The Native Americans separated the white layers of the bark and used it as a type of paper and also to make lightweight canoes. The canoes were created by stretching Canoe Birch *Betula papyrifea* bark over northern white cedar frames. The seams were sewn with a thread made from tamarack roots and the finished vessel was caulked with pine or fir resin.

An oil taken from birch bark is used to make leather durable, and the oil of birch tar is a natural insect repellent.

The inner bark of the Canoe Birch dyes wool light brown. Add blue vitriol to make a green dye. The roots of the Black Birch will give wool a reddish-brown color.

If your garden or field tends to get soggy, planting a stand of birches will help dry the soil.

Herbal Uses

Birch is a tree whose strong properties are available year round. Birch leaves are best when used fresh. Make an infusion by steeping one teaspoon of leaves in one cup of water for thirty minutes. Drink two cups per day to heal mouth sores and to break up stones in the kidney or bladder. (If you know you have large stones please see a physician. Birch would be appropriate for small stones or sediment.)

Birch bark yields an oil that is astringent and beneficial to skin conditions such as eczema and psoriasis. It has been used to treat non-hereditary baldness as well. Make an infusion of the twigs, leaves, and bark and put it in your bath water to dry and heal moist skin eruptions. (I've seen it work nicely on poison ivy.)

Birch tea, which is made by simmering the inner bark or by infusing the young leaves, is useful to ease gout and rheumatism. It also has sedative qualities that make it a valuable sleep aid. It is high in potassium which acts with sodium in the body to regulate pH levels and maintain the balance of fluids both inside and outside of the body's cells.

The Black Birch is used to heal urinary problems and to expel worms. A tea of the inner bark makes an astringent mouthwash for mouth sores and it will benefit diarrhea, rheumatism, and boils. Simmer the bark lightly (do not boil) using one tablespoon to each half cup of water. After ten minutes turn off the flame and allow the brew to steep for two hours.

The young shoots and leaves of birches are used to make a tonic laxative (one that heals as it eases constipation, unlike commercial chemical laxatives which do nothing to improve the health of the lower bowel). The leaves have diuretic qualities, and the inner bark is used to treat fevers. Gather the fresh sap in summer to expel excess fluid and treat oedema.

Birch buds are tinctured in alcohol for out-of-season use. Colds, rheumatic conditions, stomach ulcers and pains, liver and gall bladder conditions and kidney and bladder stones will be benefited by this blood purifying remedy.

Birch charcoal should be swallowed when poison has been consumed because it is an absorbent. It is also helpful for indigestion with bloating.

In northern European and Slavic countries, birch has long been used in conjunction with steam baths and saunas. Once perspiration has begun, a "birch broom," or a leafy branch is used to flail the body and stimulate the skin. Similarly, two to five pounds of the leaves and twigs can be simmered in a cotton cloth or pillow case, and then added, along with the water, to a hot bath. This bath is repeated twice a week for fifteen weeks to benefit both internal and external conditions.

The versatile birch is an excellent wild food whose leaves, twigs, and inner bark are rich in vitamins A, B1, B2, C, and E. To make a delicious beverage tea, gather the leaves, twigs, or inner bark of the Black or Yellow Birch, chop, and cover them with hot water or hot birch sap. The liquid should never boil as it will lose its volatile oils and its delicate wintergreen flavor.

Birch syrup is not as sweet as maple syrup, but it is easier to get as the sap flows more freely. It is ready for tapping about one month after the maples.

To gather the sap, take an elder or dogwood sapling branch and cut it into five inch pieces. Hollow the piece by removing the pith, and sharpen one of its end with a knife. Drill a half inch hole about four inches deep, sloping slightly downward, into the sunny side of the tree. Gently tap the spigot into the hole, and hang a bucket, or tin can with a wire handle, from the spout. A bucket could also be placed on the ground directly under the spout. Drink the sap fresh, or boil it to make syrup. Sixteen gallons may be drawn from a large tree without harming it.

Black (Sweet Birch) Birch Beer
> *5 gallons Black Birch sap*
> *a 4 or 5 inch piece of ginger root*
> *1 gallon honey*
> *1/2 lemon sliced*
> *1 oz. yeast, softened on a piece of toast*
> *2 tablespoons cloves*

Bring the sap to a boil and add the honey. Boil for fifteen minutes and cool. Pour into a crock or large glass bottle (the kind found in old fashioned water coolers works very well). When the mixture is barely warm, float the yeast topped toast on it and add the ginger, lemon, and cloves. Cover with a cloth and allow to "work" for ten days. Strain and pour into bottles. Let the bottles stand unstoppered for two days, then cap tightly. It will be ready for use in two months.

Euell Gibbons the well known author and naturalist who is best remembered for his books on wild edible plants, says that the bark of the stump and roots has the best flavor. This can be gathered in areas where logging operations are already in progress. (Otherwise you would have to kill a tree!) Carefully dry the pieces in early summer or spring, and store in airtight jars for year round use.

People who resonate with the birch are intelligent and devoted to the causes they believe in. They want those around them to feel comfortable, and they look for ways to encourage growth in others. They are concerned about advancing public welfare. They become teachers, lawyers, business leaders, and artists.

Magical Uses

In the world of tree magic, birch is known as the Lady of the Woods. It is a tree of Venus, and its element is Water. It is also sacred to Thor. To communicate with the Goddess, meditate in a grove of birch. You will incur Her displeasure, however, if you cut the bark from a living tree. If you have need of the bark, wait until a tree has been chosen by Thor and is struck by lightning. You may then safely gather its bark for parchment.

In the Nordic tradition, Byarka (birch) is the symbol of the Earth Mother, and represents the feminine powers of growth, healing, and the natural world. Her strength is the ability to care for and support others, and to cultivate unconditional love for all beings.

Because of her healing qualities, birch wood is the wood of choice for Rune magic. To make a set of runes for divination, enter a birch wood during the waxing moon. When you find a suitable tree branch, call on Odin and Byarka to inspire your work. Place your left hand on the tree and ask if she is willing to give of herself to you. If the tree accepts, present her with a small gift—something from your heart such as a truly beautiful stone, or a shell, or some herbs and flowers that you have grown yourself. I know of one person who built a special bird house to hang in the tree to provide companionship.

When you have selected your branch, saw it off and take it to a dry place. You will need to seal the cut end with wax so that the wood does not dry too quickly. After about a month you can saw the branch into sections to make your runes. Sand the pieces and carve them, then place them in a special pouch which has been purified by smoke offerings.

Birch wood has the qualities of purification, exorcism, and protection. Birch twigs are traditionally used to make witch's brooms. Gently tapping a person or animal with a birch twig drives out negative energies or "spirits." Cradles are made from birch wood to protect newborns from psychic harm.

The Native Americans believe the birch conveys the essence of support. Birches grow in groves and seem to be joined at the roots. Thus they symbolize gentle people who enjoy being joined to others—people who are devoted and make good allies. Birch, with its clean and stylish grace, displays a beauty that sustains and supports those around it.

In Slavic countries the "Lieschi" or "Genii of the Forests" were said to live in the tops of birch trees. They could change their shape at will, and, while wandering the forests, would become as tall as trees, but, when inhabiting the plains, they were as small as a blade of grass.

Another old tradition states that trees can be protected from storms by tying a red ribbon around them. An old Russian tradition imparts that a red ribbon hung from a birch stem wards off the evil eye. A Russian tale tells how a birch tree showed its gratitude to a young girl who tied red thread around it by saving her from the abuses of her stepmother.

In yet another story, a young shepherdess was spinning in a birch wood when a wild woman appeared to her and forced her to dance for three days and nights. As the dancing stopped, the wool was magically spun and the shepherdess was paid with a pocket full of birch leaves that later turned into gold coins.

The birch tree is the national symbol of Estonia. The people speak of a peasant who awakened a stranger sleeping under a birch tree just as a storm was about to break. In gratitude, the stranger told the peasant that if he was ever far from home, and feeling homesick, he would see a crooked birch. He should strike the tree and ask: "Is the crooked one at home?"

Years later, when the peasant found himself serving as a soldier in Finland, he felt sad and homesick. Suddenly he saw the crooked birch, and, remembering the stranger's words, he struck it and asked, "Is the crooked one at home?" The stranger suddenly appeared before him, invoked a familiar spirit, and asked it to take the soldier home with his knapsack full of silver.

Birch is the tree to select for the undertaking of new

projects. The birch month (see Beith in the Celtic tree calendar at the end of the book) immediately follows Samhain, the Celtic new year. Her clean white bark is easily seen and makes a clear marker in a thickly grown forest. She will point the way to a clear purpose and a fresh start in life.

To me, nothing else about a tree is so remarkable
as the extreme delicacy of the mechanisms
by which it grows and lives... So it looks as though
the tree was almost made of matter and spirit, like man;
the ether with its vibrations, on the one hand,
and the earth with its inorganic compounds, on the other...
— John Burroughs

Loveliest of trees, the cherry now
Is hung with bloom along the bough,
And stands about the woodland ride
Wearing white for Eastertide.

Now, of my threescore years and ten,
Twenty will not come again,
And take from seventy springs a score,
It only leaves me fifty more.

And since to look at things in bloom
Fifty springs are little room,
About the woodlands I will go
To see the cherry hung with snow.
— A. E. Housman

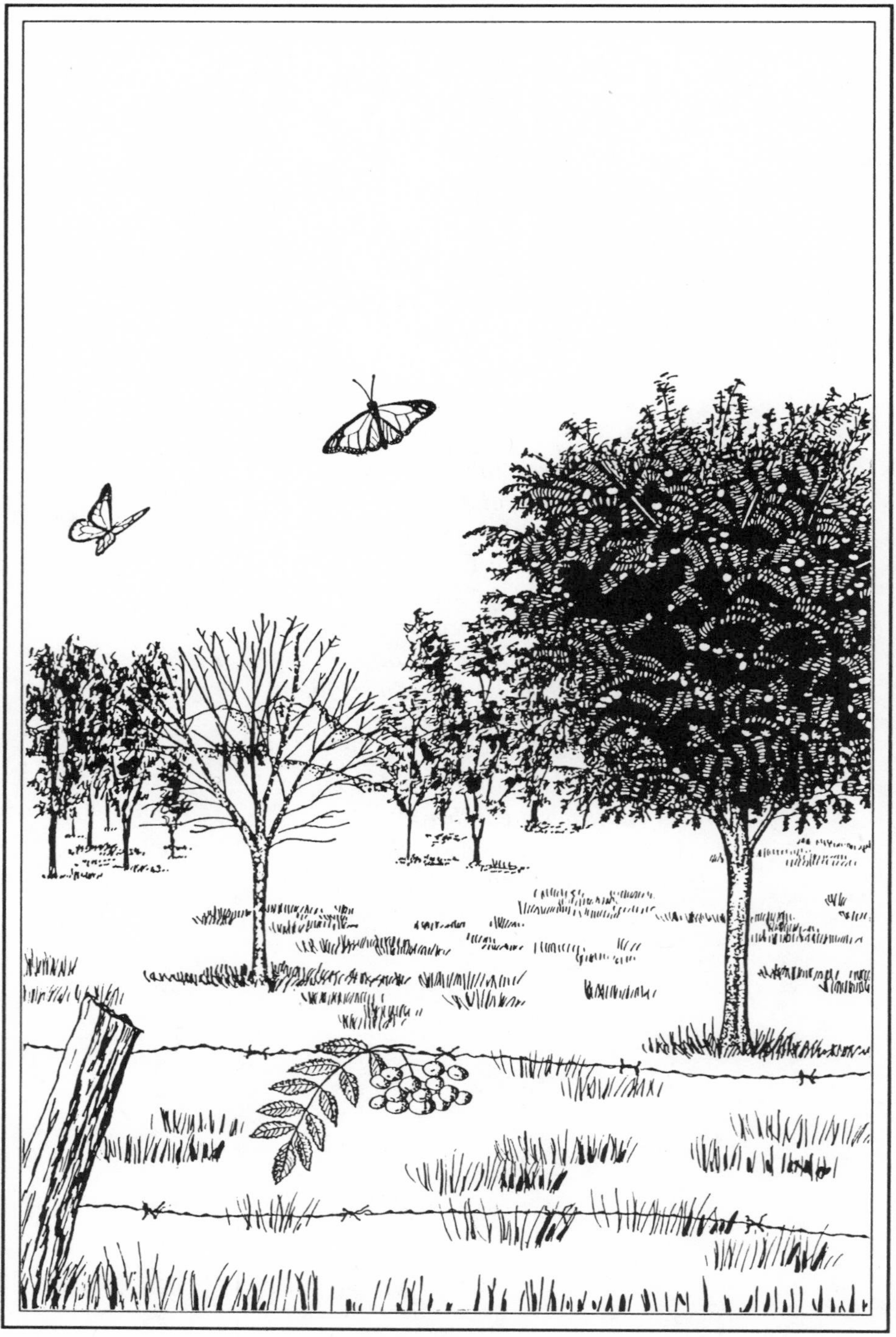

European Mountain Ash

Rowan
Woe to Those with No Rowan Tree Near

AMERICAN MOUNTAIN ASH/ROWAN *(Sorbus americana)*
A small, shrubby native of northeastern North America, it grows to thirty feet, with a spreading crown, or as a shrub with many stems, showy white flowers, and bright red berries. It usually has a trunk diameter of eight inches. The leaves grow pinnately, are six to eight inches long, and compound. The lanceolate leaflets are up to four inches long, up to one inch wide, and saw-toothed. The leaves are paler beneath and yellow in autumn. The bark is pale gray, smooth or scaly, and the twigs reddish brown. The flowers are numerous, a quarter of an inch wide with five white petals. They grow in clusters of three to five in late spring. The fruit is small, matures in autumn, has a bitter pulp, and it resembles clusters of small bright red apples. It favors moist valleys in coniferous forests from Newfoundland to western Ontario, and from Illinois to Georgia. It grows in altitudes to 6000 feet in the south.

EUROPEAN MOUNTAIN ASH/ROWAN *(Sorbus aucuparia)*
It was introduced to America in colonial times from Europe and Eurasia. It is open, spreading, and has a rounded crown. It attains a height of forty feet with a trunk diameter of one foot. The leaves are pinnately compound, four to eight inches long, with nine to seventeen leaflets that are one to two inches long and less than an inch wide. The leaves are oblong or lanceolate, saw-toothed except at the base, dull green above, with white hairs beneath, and they turn red in the fall. The bark is dark gray and smooth with horizontal lines and it is very aromatic. The flowers grow in three to six inch clusters of seventy-five to one hundred flowers, and are small with five white petals. The fruit resembles clusters of small bright red apples. They are five sixteenths of an inch wide with a bitter pulp, and they mature in spring. Rowan favors roadsides and thickets from southeastern Alaska to southern Canada, Newfoundland to Maine, and Minnesota to California.

The rowan tree is a royal herb of the sun whose orange berries may have been a significant source of sustenance for our ancestors. Through the long snows of winter, rowan berries supplied birds and humans with large quantities of vitamins A and C. The berries of the rowan tree are an important food for grouse, cedar waxwings, grosbeaks, and other birds. Moose eat the leaves, twigs, and inner bark.

The Latin species name means "to catch birds." In former times, the berries were used to make bird lime which was smeared on branches to catch birds. The word "rowan" comes from the Scandinavian raun (red) in reference to the berries.

Practical Uses

Grow a rowan as an ornamental for its beautiful flowers and fruit, and your garden will soon be filled with grateful birds.

Rowan wood is a strong building material suitable for heavy duty use such as fence posts and ship building.

Rowan bark will dye wool gray.

Herbal Uses

The fresh juice of the rowan berry (American Mountain Ash berries can be used as a substitute) is a laxative, and it makes an excellent gargle for sore throats, inflamed tonsils, and hoarseness. Rowan berry jam can be kept on hand all year and is a remedy for diarrhea. An infusion of the berries benefits hemorrhoids and strangury (stoppage of urine).

To prepare the berries, soak one teaspoon of the dried fruit in one cup of water for ten hours. The dose is one cup per day. If fresh berries are available, the juice can be given in teaspoonful doses as needed. Please note: the berries are bitter.

To make rowan berry jam, use one part berries to half a part sugar. In cases of mild diarrhea, one tablespoon three to five times a day will offer relief.

Dried berries can be substituted for coffee beans and were used in the past to flavor liqueurs and cordials. The ancient Welsh included them in a recipe for ale.

The decoction of the bark is an astringent that will be valuable in cases of loose bowels and as a douche for vaginal irritations. The fresh bark should be tinctured in alcohol and extracted for eight days. This will produce a fever remedy that resembles quinine.

Homeopaths use Mountain Ash and rowan (Pyrus) for eye irritation, feelings of constriction around the waist, sensations of cold water in the stomach that extend to the esophagus, spasmic pains in the uterus, heart and bladder, and for neuralgia and gout.

Magical Uses

The rowan is known as a tree of protection and it comes under the dominion of Thor and Rauni, the Finno-Ugric Earth Mother (also known as Akka and Maa-Emoineh). Rowan is an herb of Uranus and its element is Fire. Its healing energy imparts psychic and supernatural powers.

Rowan branches may be used to dowse for water, and they are sometimes made into magic wands. Walking sticks made of rowan wood will protect the wanderer from harm, and carrying rowan on sea voyages is said to protect the craft from storms.

Gather rowan branches at Beltane (May Day), bind them with yards of red thread or wool, and place them prominently in your window. Twigs may be fashioned into an equal-armed cross, bound with red thread, and hung indoors or placed on an altar. In the Scottish Highlands, a small rowan cross is sewn into garments as a protective charm. A rhyming verse sung over the branches will enhance their effectiveness.

In Scotland, rowan trees were often planted near houses as a protection from lightning and other evil influences. Plant one in honor of a new home, or when you start your family.

Rowan trees planted on graves prevent the haunting of the place by the one who has "passed over."

Rowan trees are often found near stone circles in Scotland. In such locations, the trees will have great power, perhaps because of their intimate association with the fairies attracted to the celebrations held within the circles.

Rowan berries have a small pentagram (five pointed star) at the point where they are joined to the stalk. This ancient symbol of protection is the emblem of the perfected human—

each point of the star refers to arms, legs, and the head.

Rowan berries and leaves are dried and burned as incense to invoke spirits, familiars, spirit guides, elementals, and the great Goddess. The same berries can be used to banish undesirable entities and thoughtforms. The berries and bark are added to healing mixtures and sewn into sachets. They bring health, power, luck, and success.

Rowan wood was burned by the druids of opposing armies to summon spirits to take part in battle. In the legend of Fraoth, rowan berries were guarded by a dragon and were said to give sustenance equal to nine meals. They could heal the wounded, and were said to add a year to a life.

Great stands of rowan, which were used as places of oracle and divination, stood on the Amber Islands of the Baltic. In former times, rowan twigs were used to dowse for metal just as hazel was used to divine for water.

In county Sligo, Ireland, people say that the rowan originally came from Fairyland (the Land of Promise). This land was the home of the DéDannan—the fairy folk of Eire. When they came to Ireland, they brought with them rowan berries, one of which fell to the ground in the Wood of Dubhros. From this berry grew a tree which embodied all the virtues of the rowan. Its berries tasted like honey, and all who ate them felt cheerful and young.

Tree at my window, window tree,
My sash is lowered when night comes on;
But let there never be curtain drawn
Between you and me.

Vague dream-head lifted out of the ground,
And thing next most diffuse to cloud,
Not all your light tongues talking aloud
Could be profound.

But, tree, I have seen you taken and tossed,
And if you have seen me when I slept,
You have seen me when I was taken and swept
And all but lost.

That day she put our heads together,
Fate had her imagination about her,
Your head so much concerned with outer,
Mine with inner, weather.

— Robert Frost

Common Apple

Apple
Apple, the Tree of Love

APPLE AND CRAB APPLE *(Malus spp.)*
Apples and Crab Apples are both of the genus Malus which includes deciduous trees that bear small, five petaled, rosaceous flowers, and fruits that range from pea sized to apples four inches in diameter. Any fruit with less than a two inch diameter is described as a Crab Apple. The leaves of apples are alternate, two to four inches long, and up to two and a half inches wide. Those of the Crab Apple are shorter, narrower, and more delicate. Crab Apples tend to be small trees of fifteen to twenty-five feet. Not all Crab Apples are edible when raw, but all can be made into jellies and jams. Many species of apples have been introduced to the United States and Canada especially along watercourses which are a means of spreading the seeds.

COMMON APPLE OR WILD APPLE *(Malus sylvestris)*
Native to Europe and Western Asia, the apple has been cultivated since ancient times. Jonathan Chapman (1774-1845), known as "Johnny Appleseed," distributed seeds for fifty years from Pennsylvania to Illinois. The tree has a short trunk, rounded, broad crown, and attains a height of forty feet. Its trunk diameter is one to two feet. The leaves are up to three and a half inches long, up to two and a quarter inches wide, elliptical or ovate, wavy and saw-toothed with a hairy leaf stalk. They are green above and covered with gray hairs beneath. The bark is gray, scaly, and fissioned. The flowers bloom in early spring, are white with a pink blush, have five rounded petals, and are one and a quarter inch wide. The fruit is two to three and a half inches wide, red to yellow, with a sweet pulp and a star shaped core. The fruits bear up to ten seeds and mature in summer. Apple favors moist soil near roadsides and open areas.

There was a time when every farmstead in northern Europe and north eastern America made its own apple cider, and apple pies and pastries have been a popular food for centuries. In Tudor England, apple pies were flavored with cinnamon and ginger and dyed yellow with saffron.

Apple butter is a traditional New England confection that was made in the colonial period by boiling apples in a large cauldron of cider until they were reduced to a thick paste. This was then flavored with allspice.

At Yuletide, there was an old custom of "wassailing the orchard trees." In Devonshire, England, a farm family and its hired help would go to the orchard after supper bearing cider and cakes. The cakes were placed in the boughs of the oldest and best trees, and cider was poured on the trees as a libation. (Some say that the cider was a substitute for the blood used in earlier times as a form of ritual fertilization.)

Roasted apples were floated in the cider, and were given to the trees with the libation. Trees which were poor bearers were not honored with the drink. After thanking the trees and offering a toast to their health, the farmers would solicit the trees to continue to produce abundantly. Those standing by would cheer and make noise with noisemakers.

Samhain, or Hallowe'en, is the traditional time to "bob for apples," but those who consider the day a spiritual occasion (Samhain is also the old Celtic new year's day) place apples upon their altar.

At "la mas nbhal," Ireland's "feast of the apple gathering" which was also celebrated on Hallowe'en, a hot spiced drink made of ale, wine, or cider with apples and bits of toast floating in it was served. Each person who drank the beverage would take out an apple and give a blessing to the assembled folk before eating it.

To the Native Americans, the apple tree is a symbol of honor. They respect it as a being who provides food, living places, and medicine for many living creatures. Dependable and not too tall or demanding, it leaves enough sunlight for other creatures and plants to grow.

The apple tree wears the color green to show its willingness to grow, yellow to reveal its love, and red to represent faith.

Apple blossoms convey sweetness and love with their delicate color and scent.

Apple trees seem to seek popularity, sharing their gifts and talents with others. They teach us about dependability, sincerity, healthy attitudes, and the ethics of caring for others as much as we care for ourselves. Apples are smallish trees that

grow within human reach. They thrive on human companionship and feel their best when petted and pruned.

Practical Uses

Apple wood is used for small decorative carvings and for
gunstocks and inlays. The bark of the tree gives a tan color to
alum mordanted wool. Crab Apples make a pink dye for alum
mordanted wool.

Herbal Uses

The original wild apple was the Crab Apple. Today there
are over 2000 varieties available. Apples are truly a way to
"keep the doctor away." They contain magnesium, iron, potassium, carbohydrates, and vitamins C, B, and B2. Apples are
rich in phosphates, the great tissue builders of the body, each
of which carries four atoms of oxygen. Iron phosphate, an
oxygen carrier, potassium phosphate, a brain and nerve
builder, magnesium phosphate, a muscle builder, and sodium
phosphate, an alkalinic solvent and stabilizer, are all found in
the apple. The apple also provides a number of other oxygen
carriers. Oxygen is a great purifier, cleanser, vitalizer, antiseptic, neutralizer of acids, disinfectant and stimulant to the heart,
nerves and brain.

Apples are peeled and grated to treat diarrhea (a two day
apple fast of unripe apples is recommended). Apples eaten
whole have a laxative effect. Apples benefit the liver and aid
digestion. Their sugar passes easily into the blood stream so
they are a good source of quick, clean energy. There is
evidence that eating a ripe apple at night can ease insomnia—
probably because of the cleansing effects on the liver and
bowel.

Baked apples are used as a poultice for sore throats,
fevers, and inflammations. Stewed apples cleanse the bowels.
Applesauce left out overnight and eaten the next day
replenishes intestinal flora. (This will be especially useful after
a round of antibiotics which are known to destroy the "good
bugs" along with the "bad" in the intestinal tract.)

Apples have been used to reduce fevers and neutralize

toxins in the blood. Raw apples benefit the gums and reduce cavities by clearing deposits from the teeth.

A study at Michigan State University found that students who ate two apples a day had fewer tensions, headaches, and emotional upsets by a twelve to one ratio than those who ate none.

Dried apple peel can make a tea which eases rheumatic conditions. Two teaspoons of dried peel may be steeped in one cup of hot water for twenty minutes. One to three cups per day is the dose. Apple peel eaten in small amounts can ease heartburn. In cases of diarrhea, apple peel can be simmered in boiled milk. The dose is one warm, half cup every hour.

The root bark contains phlorizin, a bitter principle that surpasses quinine for treating intermittent fevers. The bark contains quercin—a bitter astringent found also in oak trees. The dose is one to four ounces of the infused bark.

Apple wine is aged two years to make a tonic for the whole body.

Caution: Apple seeds can be poisonous if eaten in significant quantities. About five to twenty-five seeds (they vary in strength) can harm a young child if the ingested seed capsules are broken. An adult can eat several hundred without any ill side-effects.

Apple blossom perfume is soothing for asthma and respiratory problems. According to Dr. Edward Shook, the scent adds ozone to the oxygen of the air and provides relief to those suffering from asthma and other respiratory diseases. Apple blossom honey is one of the healthiest, purest honeys available. I've sampled some that was almost as clear as water and tasted like delicate perfume.

Apple cider is a valuable herbal remedy. By itself it reduces the acidity of the stomach, clears gas, and cleans the liver. As an intestinal germicide, apple cider inhibits putrefaction. The malic acid it contains is slightly diuretic and helps the kidneys to expel uric acid wastes. (Uric acid has been detected in patients who suffer from gouty conditions and it is also a problem when the diet is rich in red meats.) In countries where unsweetened cider is a common beverage, stones or calculi are unknown. One cup of cider three of four times a day is recommended for the above conditions.

By adding garlic and horseradish to cider, a potent panacea is created that can benefit ulcerations, boils, acne, abscesses, tumors, eczema, psoriasis, lupus, internal infections, athletes foot, ophthalmia, mastoiditis, bone necrosis, and pus and inflammation in the lung. To create this concoction, add eight ounces of fresh garlic juice and one ounce of grated horseradish to two quarts of apple cider. Allow the mixture to stand for twelve hours in a warm place, and then twelve hours in a cool place. Shake at intervals, strain, and bottle. Store in a cool, dark location. Take one tablespoon three or four times a day between meals.

Swollen glands, infections, tumors, bone growths, ulcers, skin diseases, sore throats, sebaceous cysts, infected wounds, carbuncles, boils, acne, eczema, and lupus will all benefit from external application of this mixture. If the application causes pain, the affected part should be first covered with castor oil. It will also treat sciatica, rheumatism, and paralysis. Equal parts of glycerine are added to treat edematous tissue.

Apple cider or natural, unpasteurized apple juice blended with celery, beet, and carrot juices benefits skin problems, can aid in weight loss programs, and can clear catarrh from the lungs.

Apples blended with cucumber juice clean the kidney and bladder, and will help purify the intestines, lungs, and skin.

One part apple cider vinegar mixed with one part water is useful as a face rinse and helps to restore blemished skin. This can also be used as a hair rinse that will promote the proper pH of the hair and scalp. Blondes should only use white vinegar.

Magical Uses

The apple is one of the oldest plants for which we have archaeological evidence. We know from excavations that stone age Swiss lake dwellers used apples. Despite popular misconceptions the apple is not mentioned in the Biblical account of Adam and Eve.

One of the twelve labors of Hercules was to steal the golden apples, said to bestow virtue and immortality, from the gardens of the Hesperides.

The Greeks believed the gardens of the Hesperides were another Eden and that they were located somewhere on an island off the west coast of Africa. Titaea, an Earth Goddess, was among the Deities who attended Zeus and Hera's wedding ceremony. As her gift, she manifested a tree with golden apples. The Hesperides, who were assigned to care for the tree, were constantly tempted to partake of its fruits. To protect them, the serpent Ladon was placed by the tree. After slaying Ladon, Hercules stole a few apples which were later returned, with the help of Athena, to the Hesperides.

The ancient Greeks attributed the Trojan war to the Apple of Discord that was tossed before the assembled Gods by Eris. On it was written: "for the fairest." Hera, Athena, and Aphrodite each claimed the apple for themselves, and Paris, Prince of Troy, was commanded to make the choice. Hera offered wealth and power, and Athena fame and wisdom. Aphrodite won, however, with a promise to give Paris the most beautiful woman alive—Helen. Paris managed to entice Helen away from her husband and took her to Troy. Thus apples are symbolic of choice and beauty.

Hippomenes was a young Greek who charmed Atalanta by beating her in a foot race. He was helped by Aphrodite who gave him three golden apples with which to distract her during the contest.

Meditate on apple wood when you contemplate a decision with several attractive alternatives. Hold it to your heart and ask which outcome you truly desire. Which would be the most life enhancing for you? Then realize that in making that choice, other desirable options will need to be released with a blessing.

Apples are sacred to Venus/Aphrodite, Hercules, Diana, Iduna, King Arthur, Dionysus, Olwen, Apollo, Hera, Athena, and Zeus. They are known as an herb of Venus, and are of the Water element. In rituals to honor Venus/Aphrodite, juice and apples are shared and offered. Apple seeds and bark may be burned as incense.

August 13th was Diana's feast day in Greece and Venus' in Rome. The ritual meal included an apple bough laden with fruit.

Apple wood was traditionally used to make wands for love magic. Apple peel can be dried and placed in sachets to attract love, while the fruit itself can be eaten to ensure fertility. Apples also strengthen the powers of healing, garden magic, and immortality. They promote relaxation when added to the bath, and apple blossom oil is used to anoint candles in love magic rituals. In magical spells, the juice can be used in place of wine.

In the Scandinavian Edda, it is told that the goddess Iduna presented her magical apples to the Gods for rejuvenation. (Considering the considerable healing powers of the apple and its juice this story begins to look quite plausible!)

According to Greek legend, carrying an apple branch that bears flowers, buds, and fruit will enable one to enter the underworld.

Arthur's island of Avalon was said to be covered with apple trees, and, in the traditional English ballad of Thomas the Rhymer, Thomas was warned by the Queen of the Fairies not to eat the apples or pears in her garden as they were the food of the dead. Consuming the fruit prevented any return to the land of the living.

Two simple spells keep your love warm: Cut an apple in half and share it with your lover, or hold an apple until it is warm and hand it to your intended partner. If they eat it, your love will be returned.

If you have an orchard, bury thirteen leaves from your trees after the harvest to ensure a bountiful crop next year. Offer cider as a libation to the newly turned earth of your garden or fields.

Unicorns are fond of apples. Enter an apple orchard on a misty day and perhaps you will see one.

Bluegum Eucalyptus

Eucalyptus
Cool Eucalyptus, Tree of Blue Fire

EUCALYPTUS *(Eucalyptus amygdalina)*
The tallest tree. Native to Tasmania and Australia, it attains a height of 480 feet, exceeding even the Sequoia sempervirens. The leaves are leathery, hanging obliquely or vertically, studded with oil filled glands, lanceolate, curved, three to twelve inches long, and three inches wide. The tree flowers in November and December, and the flowers are pinkish white. The fruit capsules are three quarters of an inch wide and half globular. It favors moist, rich valleys, and wooded hillsides.

BLUE GUM TREE, EUCALYPTUS FEVER TREE
(Eucalyptus globulus)
A native of Australia, it is also cultivated in India, Europe, north and south Africa, and in the southern and western United States. The leaves are glaucous white on young plants, but mature to a dark green. They are six to twelve inches long and one and a half inches wide. The flowers are one and a half inches across, and the fruit is one inch wide. The trunk is smooth and bluish white. The tree is evergreen, fast growing, and attractive to bees. It attains a height of 300 feet. It is cultivated in low lying swampy areas where temperatures do not drop below twenty-seven degrees Fahrenheit.

The Blue Gum Tree is an Australian native that has become a welcome immigrant all over the world. In the nineteenth century, it was valued for its ability to absorb huge amounts of water which made it useful to dry up marshy, malarial districts. Prized for its ability to dry the swamps of the earth, the eucalyptus also works in human and animal systems to clean and disinfect wounds and lung conditions of all kinds.

There are over 450 distinct varieties of eucalyptus ranging from dwarf shrubs of a few feet to the towering and awesome *Eucalyptus amygdalus.* The smaller trees are often found in desert areas and produce showy blossoms of crimson and pink, yellow, green or white.

Eucalyptus buds are covered by a protective cap *operculum* which drops off to release delicate, radiating flowers.

As eucalyptus trees are some of the largest living beings inhabiting the earth today, they are well worthy of our attention and respect.

 ## Practical Uses

Eucalyptus trees have historically been harvested for the essential oils found in the leaves. These are principally the medicinal oils such as eucalyptol (cineol), the industrial oils containing terpenes, and the aromatic oils such as E. citriodora which have been distilled from the fresh foliage of several species for use in soap making and perfumes.

Eucalyptus trees are planted in marshy areas due to their powerful drying action on the soil. The tree is thus viewed as a major agent in the prevention of malaria.

Herbal Uses

The most medicinally active part of the eucalyptus plant is the oil from its leaves, which, when used with wisdom, is almost an entire pharmacy in itself. The active principle in the oil is eucalyptol (cineol), a natural disinfectant and fever reducer. Used in proper amounts, it aids digestion and increases the appetite.

A word of caution: LARGE DOSES CAN BE FATAL. The dose should never exceed more than three drops per day for an adult. Overdosing can result in kidney irritation, or even cause asphyxiation by depressing the action of the medullary center.

To use eucalyptus externally, one ounce of eucalyptus mixed with one pint of water will prevent infection when applied to wounds and ulcers. The oil has been used to treat burns and gum diseases such as pyorrhea.

A wonderful remedy for bronchitis, sinusitis, and microbic diseases of the lung consists of three drops of eucalyptus (no more) mixed with two drops of peppermint oil and the juice of half a lemon in a cup of steaming water. Inhale the steam and then gradually sip the cooled brew. *Under no circumstances* should more than one cup a day of this preparation be ingested.

Eucalyptus makes a fine sore throat gargle (place a few drops in warm water). Eucalyptus oil is a powerful antiseptic forming ozone upon exposure to air. It is a disinfectant which destroys lower life forms such as oxygen dependent bacteria. Place a few drops in your vaporizer to ease asthma attacks. Two drops in water can be taken twice a day when gonorrhea is suspected. Eucalyptus in water prevents distemper when a drop or two a day is given to animals in the spring. In addition, the oil is effective as a tonic for humans when epidemics of flu and pneumonia are moving through the population.

Eucalyptus has been used in repeated small doses to treat malaria, recurrent chills, and leukemia. One third cup of water mixed with no more than one drop of the oil and taken three times a day stimulates heart action.

Homeopaths use a tincture of the fresh leaf of the eucalyptus as a stimulating expectorant and diaphoretic. It is especially valuable for influenza, internal and external hemorrhages, typhoid, exhaustion, lung conditions, genito-urinary and gastro-intestinal infections and pain.

Magical Uses

Eucalyptus, an herb of the moon, belongs to the Air element. Not surprisingly, it is thought of as an herb of healing and protection.

Hang branches of eucalyptus over the sick bed, or wear the leaves and pods in medicine bags and as necklaces. Surround yourself with the sight and smell of eucalyptus to ward off illness.

When working magic for a sore throat, it is good to remember that the color of the throat chakra is blue. Wear blue cloth around the neck and have a blue cloth and candles surrounded by eucalyptus leaves on the altar.

Slippery Elm

Elm
Elm Tree, the Elf Friend

AMERICAN ELM *(Ulmus americana)*
Native to central and eastern North America, it was once common on city streets and lawns but has been decimated by a fungus spread by European Elm bark beetles. A large, usually forked tree with spreading and drooping branches, it is often wider than high. It attains a height of one hundred feet with a trunk diameter of four feet or more. The leaves grow in two rows, are three to six inches long and one to three inches wide, elliptical, long and pointed, doubly saw-toothed with parallel side veins, and turning bright yellow in the fall. The bark is gray and deeply furrowed with broad, scaly ridges. The flowers are an eighth of an inch long and greenish in early spring. The keys (one seeded, winged fruits of trees such as the elm) are elliptical, flat, and they mature in spring. The tree favors moist valleys and flood plains in hardwood forest areas. Its range is from southeastern Saskatchewan to Cape Breton, and Florida to central Texas. It grows in altitudes to 2500 feet.

ENGLISH OR EUROPEAN ELM *(Ulmus procera = Ulmus campestris)*
Native to England and western Europe and brought to America in colonial times. It has a tall, straight trunk, and spreading, almost upright branches. It attains a height of eighty feet with a trunk diameter of three feet. The leaves grow in two rows, are two to three and a quarter inches long and up to two inches wide, elliptical, long-pointed at the tip, doubly saw-toothed with an uneven base, have ten to twelve veins to a side, and they are darker green above. The bark is gray and furrowed into plates. The flowers are an eighth of an inch, dark red, and they appear in early spring. The fruit are half-inch greenish keys that mature in spring. The tree favors moist soils of roadsides and forest borders.

SLIPPERY ELM *(Ulmus fulva = Ulmus rubra)*
A broad, open, flat topped tree with large leaves and spreading branches. It attains a height of seventy feet with a trunk

diameter of three feet. The leaves grow in two rows, are four to seven inches long and two to three inches wide, elliptical, long-pointed with unequal sides, doubly saw-toothed with parallel veins, rough on top, with soft hairs beneath. The dark, brown bark is deeply furrowed. The flowers are an eighth of an inch, greenish, and grow along the twigs in early spring. The keys, appearing in the spring, are light green. The Slippery Elm favors the moist soils of flood plains and the drier areas in hardwood forests. Its range is from southwestern Maine to southern Ontario, and central Texas to northern Florida. It grows in altitudes to 2000 feet.

ROCK OR CORK ELM *(Ulmus thomasii)*
A native North American tree with a straight trunk and a narrow crown of short, drooping branches. It grows to a height of one hundred feet with a trunk diameter of one to three feet. The leaves are two to three and a half inches long and one to two inches wide, elliptical, long-pointed with a rounded, unequal base, doubly saw-toothed with parallel veins, dark green above, and paler beneath. The leaves turn yellow in the fall. The bark is gray with deep furrows and ridges. The flowers are an eighth of an inch wide, greenish and they appear in the early spring. It produces elliptical, flat keys in the spring. It favors moist soils, or dry and rocky uplands, limestone bluffs, and hardwood forests. Its range is from southern Ontario to western New England, and south to Tennessee, Kansas, and Minnesota. It grows in altitudes to 2500 feet.

The European Elm was called elven in ancient Britain due to its popularity with the elves. For those of you who desire contact with wood elves, I have it on good authority that they love music and singing. Pick a secluded forest area, build a small fire, and prepare for an all night vigil of gentle music, storytelling, and light refreshment. They will generally appear towards dawn, or when they feel sure of your intentions.

Practical Uses

Elm wood is used for furniture, panelling, and containers. The Rock Elm or Cork Elm has a hard, tough wood that makes it suitable for farm tools. In the last century, the wood was exported to England to build wooden battleships and sailing vessels.

Herbal Uses

The European or English Elm is generally used for medicinal purposes. If you know of an area where a tree has fallen, you can gather the leaves and bark and tincture them in vinegar for two weeks. (Grind the leaves with a mortar and pestle or an electric blender, chop the bark as finely as you can and cover with cider vinegar. Let the mix sit for up to two weeks, shaking it at intervals.) The vinegar tincture is applied to skin diseases and eruptions. The leaves, bark, and root are simmered in water for twenty minutes and added to bath water to help heal broken bones.

A good elm to use in herbal medicine is the Slippery Elm, which is a smaller variety. It possesses a very nutritious inner bark which is soothing to the skin and mucous membranes of the body. To identify a Slippery Elm tree, try chewing through the outer bark of a twig. The inner bark should be fragrant and glue-like.

It is best to harvest the bark in the spring from a tree which is at least ten years old. Unfortunately, since the wood has no commercial value, harvested trees are usually left to die. In extreme emergencies, the inner bark can be eaten right from the tree—if you are lost in the woods you might eat some and send a fervent prayer of thanks to the Tree Spirit for its noble sacrifice. Slippery Elm is readily available from health food stores and herbalists.

For babies who cannot tolerate cow's milk, Slippery Elm makes a wholesome substitute. Mash one teaspoon of the powdered bark into a paste, add cold water, and then gradually stir in a pint of boiling water. Besides being rich in calcium, the drink eases insomnia and is soothing to the stomach and bowels. Sesame seeds or almonds softened in water may be blended into the liquid.

A type of pudding is made by beating one teaspoon of the powdered bark with one egg. Slowly stir in boiled milk and sweetener such as raw honey. Cinnamon, nutmeg, lemon rind, or almond extract may also be added for flavor.

Slippery Elm ingested three times a day is beneficial for

gastritis, colitis, enteritis, bronchitis, coughs, and bleeding from the lungs.

For coughs, make an infusion, add a pinch of cayenne and some lemon juice with honey to taste. Take in frequent small doses up to a total of one pint per day. This formula is also good for typhoid fever. The dose is two tablespoons per hour or as much as the patient desires.

Slippery Elm is useful in enemas. For cystitis, use one ounce of the powdered bark added to one pint of boiling water, strained and cooled. (For best results, add twenty drops, or one teaspoon, each of echinacea, golden seal and uva ursi tinctures to the cystitis mix.) To ease diarrhea, make an enema solution of Slippery Elm, powdered bayberry, and skullcap. Pour boiling water over the whole mixture and steep for half an hour. One teaspoon of myrrh, echinacea, or yarrow tincture may be added when it cools. For constipation, combine half a pint of warm milk with one ounce of the powdered bark. Water and olive oil complete the enema mixture. To expel tapeworms, mix two ounces of Slippery Elm with one drachma of male fern oil, add water, and use in an enema bag.

Slippery Elm is first class poultice material. During the Revolutionary War, surgeons used poultices of the bark for gunshot wounds with excellent results. The poultice may be applied to wounds, boils, ulcers, burns, poison ivy, and skin inflammations. Mix the powdered bark with hot water to make a paste, spread on a clean cotton cloth, and wrap around the affected body part. For hairy parts of the body, smear olive oil on the poultice before applying. Leave it on for about an hour.

For severely infected wounds, mix equal parts of Slippery Elm powder, wormwood, and fine charcoal. This is said to benefit even gangrenous tissue. For rheumatism, gout, and synovitis make a poultice of equal parts Slippery Elm, wheat bran, and hot vinegar.

Elm was one of the plants chosen by Dr. Edward Bach for his flower essence therapy. Elm flower essence benefits a person who is overwhelmed by responsibilities, and feels that no matter what or how much they do, they are inadequate to accomplish the task. Dejection and exhaustion are the result. They tend to be very capable people. If they are not careful, they allow themselves to become "indispensable," thus creating emotional and physical burdens for themselves. Their great fear is that they will fail and disappoint the people who depend upon them. This state is usually temporary because these people often have an inner conviction that they are "chosen" to do the work and so they remain inspired. The positive aspect of such persons is the true inner confidence and self assurance with which they help others.

The remedy is made by infusing the flowers of the elm in sunlight for four hours. The dose is four drops, four times a day, under the tongue. (See Herbal Basics for preparation method.) Because the bark contains vanadium, a trace mineral valuable to the brain stem, the tincture of Slippery Elm has been found useful in treating manic depression.

Infusion for Slippery Elm
Steep two ounces of inner bark in one quart water that has been freshly boiled for one hour. Take one teaspoon every thirty minutes.

Decoction for Slippery Elm
Add one teaspoon inner bark to one pint just boiled water. Steep one hour then boil for a few minutes. Let stand one hour, then boil again.

Magical Uses

Because of its popularity with elves, this tree is thought to be helpful in learning to communicate with the realm of Devas and the fairies. Find a favorite elm and spend time with it. Bring it offerings of wine, mead, tobacco, coins, or sage. Share yourself, your hopes and dreams, with this tree, and when you feel a rapport, consecrate the relationship with a ritual. Once you and the tree are bonded, just enjoy the relationship.

Elm is a tree of Saturn and of the Earth element. It is especially sacred to Odin, Hoenin, and Lodr.

Tiny pieces of twig placed in a power bundle around a child's neck may produce eloquent speech in later life. The wood bound with a yellow cord and then burned will prevent gossip. A legend describes a forest of elms appearing at Orpheus's feet when he was playing the lyre, mourning the loss of Eurydice.

Sugar Maple

Maple
Sweet Maple, Tree of Friendship and Desire

NORWAY MAPLE *(Acer platanoides)*
Native to Norway, northern Poland and Lithuania, it now grows all over northern and central Europe. Also now found in eastern American cities and in the Middle West. It grows to a height of fifty feet with a trunk diameter of two feet. Its leaves are opposite, four to seven inches long, palmately five lobed, have scattered long teeth, five to seven veins from the base, and are bright yellow in autumn. The bark is gray or brown with narrow ridges. The flowers are five sixteenths of an inch with five yellow-green petals. The male and female flowers grow on separate trees in early spring before the foliage appears. The keys (winged fruit pods) are up to two inches long, paired with a long wing and flattened body, and they mature in summer. The tree thrives in polluted cities and in humid, temperate regions.

PLANETREE MAPLE *(Acer pseudoplatanus)*
Native of Europe and western Asia, it now grows in the eastern United States. A large, widely spreading tree with a rounded crown. It grows to seventy feet with a two foot trunk diameter. The leaves are palmate, five lobed with short points, wavy saw-toothed, with five veins from the base, paler underneath, and they turn brown in the fall. The bark is gray and smooth or scaly. The flowers are yellow-green, grow in clusters that are five inches long, and they bloom in early spring. The keys are paired and have an elliptical body, are light brown, and they mature in summer. The tree is tolerant of sea air and salt spray, and hardy along roadsides. It is known as the Sycamore in Europe.

RED MAPLE *(Acer rubrum)*
A native American tree introduced to Europe for furniture making. A large tree with a narrow or rounded crown. It attains a height of ninety feet with a trunk diameter of two and a half feet. The leaves are opposite, broad, ovate, two and a half to four inches long, with three shallow lobes, may have two small lobes at the base, and are saw-toothed. The flowers, fruit, leaf stalks, and fall foliage are red, orange, and yellow. The bark is

*gray and smooth, and it develops ridges as the tree ages. The
flowers are an eighth of an inch long. The male and female
blossoms grow in separate clusters, and they bloom in late
winter or early spring. The keys are reddish, up to one inch long,
one seeded with a long wing, and they mature in spring. The
tree favors stream banks, damp valleys, swampy areas, and dry
ridges in mixed hardwood forests. Its range is from Newfoundland to southern Florida, and eastern Texas to
southeastern Manitoba. It grows in altitudes to 6000 feet.*

SILVER MAPLE *(Acer saccharinum)*
*A Sugar Maple native to America. A large tree with a short
trunk, several large forks, and long, curving branches. It grows
to eighty feet and has a trunk diameter of three feet. The leaves
are opposite, four to six inches long, ovate, five lobed, long-
pointed, and doubly saw-toothed. They are silver white on the
underside, and pale yellow in the fall. The bark is gray and,
when mature, it develops long ridges. The flowers are one
quarter of an inch long with male and female in separate
clusters, and they bloom in very late spring. The keys are up to
two inches long with a broad wing, paired, light brown, one
seeded, and they mature in spring. The tree favors wet soils,
swamps, and hardwood forests. Its range is from New
Brunswick to northwestern Florida and Oklahoma, to northern
Minnesota. It grows in altitudes to 2000 feet.*

THE SUGAR MAPLE/ROCK MAPLE *(Acer saccharum)*
*A large, rounded tree that attains a height of one hundred feet
and has a trunk diameter of three feet. The leaves are opposite,
up to five and a half inches long, palmately, with five deep
pointed lobes and a few narrow teeth, five veins from the base,
and multicolored in the fall. The bark is light gray, but becomes
furrowed and ridged. The flowers are three sixteenths of an inch
long with a five lobed, bell shaped, greenish yellow calyx. The
male and female blossoms are clustered on slender stalks with
the spring leaves. The keys are paired and forking, brown, one
seeded, and mature in autumn. The tree favors moist soils from
Nova Scotia to North Carolina, and Kansas to southeastern
Manitoba. It grows in altitudes to 2500 feet in the north and
5500 feet in the south.*

As I write this chapter it is at the end of March, just after
the spring equinox. In preparation for writing this, I made

myself a sumptuous breakfast of whole grain pancakes, fresh strawberries, and the dregs of last year's maple syrup. This coming weekend I expect a fresh batch to arrive with my housemate who has been away sugaring in New Hampshire.

For how many thousands of years has this late winter ritual been enacted? Just when nature looks barest—yielding only rich crops of mud and slush—she offers her sweetest treasure. As the first warm blush of spring penetrates the frost, the sensitive maples respond and the sap flows. So, too, in the world of animals and humans. The ducks are already chasing each other around the ponds, and the song birds are pairing off for the season's first nesting.

In olden times, this was the season of Eostre, the Teutonic goddess of fertility and manifestation, whose symbols were the egg and the hare. "Animal seeds" (eggs), were painted with pictures of wishes for the coming year and were then planted in the earth. Since the egg was now deprived of the possibility of growing into a bird, its life force would instead manifest the images painted on its surface.

I enjoy seeing all the chocolate bunnies and easter eggs in dime stores and supermarkets at this time of year. How many parents realize that they are perpetuating in their children a timeless ritual of magic and fertility?

Practical Uses

Maple has a fine grained wood that is suitable for inlays and for making small objects such as cups, bowls, and wooden boxes. It is an excellent material for chairs, tables, and for use in house building. Violin cases are often fashioned out of maple. Its knotted roots are suitable for fine cabinet work. Young shoots make excellent riding crops. Maple is a good fuel and it makes a fine charcoal.

Red Maple bark imparts an olive color to alum mordanted wool and gray to wool with copperas.

Norway Maple is used for sugaring in Sweden and Norway.

Planetree Maple was formerly used for sugar production, as winter fodder for sheep, and for wood working.

Red Maple is tapped for sugar in Canada. The inner bark is boiled and mixed with sulphate of lead to make a black dye.

Silver Maple is used for furniture and construction.

The sap of Sugar or Rock Maple is boiled to make syrup. It is also used for flooring and furniture.

Herbal Uses

The young leaves of the maple can be simmered into massage oils and eaten in salads. When they are steeped into a decoction, the result is a tea that cleans the liver and spleen. Native Americans taught the white settlers to boil the bark and make a soothing wash for the eyes.

Women who have recently given birth can drink a decoction of the leaves or bark to strengthen nerves and tone muscles. Use one teaspoon of herb per each cup of water and simmer for twenty minutes. The dose is one to three cups per day between meals. (If the remedy is being taken for pain in the liver or spleen a quarter cup may be taken every hour.) The decoction of the leaves makes a good poultice for boils.

Perhaps the best known use of the maple is in the making of maple syrup. High in calcium and iron, maple syrup is an excellent sugar substitute that, unlike refined white sugar, has food value.

To gather sap for sugaring, wait until the freezing nights of early spring begin to alternate with warm, above-freezing days. During the first days of sugaring, the flow will be heaviest on the southern and western sides of the tree. Later, the northern and eastern sides will also produce.

Drive a spout of sumac or elder two inches into the trunk about three feet up from the ground. Hollow sumac and elder by using an iron rod to remove the pith from a four inch stem. The spout should point slightly downward.

Several spouts can be driven into one tree and each tree yields about fifteen to thirty gallons of sap. It takes at least thirty gallons of sap to make one gallon of syrup.

Maple trees are so sensitive to weather changes that a southwest wind, or the approach of a storm, will cause the flow to cease. The ideal climate for sugaring is a northwest wind with freezing nights and sunny days.

After collecting the sap in buckets, it is slowly boiled. Be careful that it doesn't burn. If the sap begins to boil too rapidly, a few drops of cream or a tiny pat of butter will help to slow it down. The syrup is ready to pour when a candy thermometer reads seven degrees Fahrenheit (four degrees Celsius) higher than the temperature at which it was first boiled. To make loaves of maple sugar, the boiling is continued until the sap reaches 234 degrees. Then pour it into buttered molds to harden and cool.

In Scotland, the Planetree Maple is tapped during the spring and autumn to make a kind of wine. This tree yields one ounce of sugar from each quart of sap. Its leaves are dried and fed to sheep in the winter.

Pralines

Blend three cups of syrup with one cup light cream and half a teaspoon of soda. Cook in a saucepan until the mixture forms a ball when dropped into cold water (234 degrees). Remove from the heat and add one and a half tablespoons butter and two cups pecans or other nuts. Beat for two to three minutes until it thickens. Drop onto waxed paper.

Maple Nut Candy

Butter a heavy saucepan and cook two cups of syrup until the temperature reaches 250 degrees. Pour over two stiffly beaten egg whites. Beat with an electric mixer at high speed until peaks are formed. Stir in half a cup chopped, Black Walnuts or hickory nuts. Drop on wax paper by the teaspoonful.

Maple Spruce Beer

Take twenty gallons of sap and boil to reduce it to four gallons. Pick four quarts of the new green tips of Black Spruce (Picea mariana). Pour boiling sap over the spruce twigs and steep until the sap is lukewarm. Strain into a five gallon crock and add one package of activated dry yeast moistened with a small portion of the liquid. Cover the crock with a cloth for about one week until the foaming stops and the sediment clears. Bottle and cap it. It will be ready in four weeks.

Magical Uses

Maples are an herb of Jupiter and are of the Air element. Jupiter brings expansive, happy energy to any situation and the Sweet Maples are said to bring love and prosperity to the practitioner. Use the leaves in love spells or to create financial abundance.

Traditionally, the branches are used as magic wands. Children may be passed through the branches to ensure a long and prosperous life.

The Native Americans see the maple as a tree that loves company and the attentions of human beings. Maple symbolizes positive thinking and the use of intuition. Reflected in its colorful autumn display, we can see an artistic mind that enjoys freedom and cherishes beauty. People resonating maple are quiet with a gentle generosity and enjoy being of service to their families.

By the twenty-fifth of September,
the red maples generally are beginning to be ripe…,
some…raying out regularly and finely every way,
bilaterally, like the veins of a leaf;
others of more irregular form…
concealing the trunk of a tree,
seem to rest heavily flake on flake,
like yellow and scarlet clouds, wreath upon wreath….
— Henry David Thoreau

Horse Chestnut

Chestnut
Wise Chestnut, the Tree of Quiet Mind

RED HORSE CHESTNUT *(Aesculus carnea)*
A hybrid of A. hippocastanum and A. pavia. It is valued as an ornamental. It develops flower clusters which are up to ten inches tall and colored pink to red. The foliage and the shape of the tree are similar to A. hippocastanum. It blooms in mid-May and has no striking fall foliage. Found from Missouri to Texas and from Memphis, Tennessee to northern Alabama.

HORSE CHESTNUT *(Aesculus hippocastanum)*
It is highly susceptible to blight, and its leaves are poisonous in early spring. It is native to southern Europe. It attains a height of seventy-five feet with a trunk diameter of two feet. It has a spreading, rounded crown. The leaves are opposite, grow on palmately compound stalks, are three to seven inches long with five to seven leaflets in a finger-like arrangement, saw-toothed, and paler green beneath. The bark is gray or brown, thin and smooth, and it develops scaly fissures. The flowers are one inch long, bell shaped, with four to five white petals, and have red and yellow spots on the base. In the late spring, the upright flowers cluster ten inches high. It has shiny brown poisonous seeds that mature in the late summer. The tree thrives in rich humid soil across the United States.

AMERICAN CHESTNUT *(Castanea dentata)*
Formerly an important lumber tree, it is now being decimated by the blight. Its leaves are medicinal and found growing from old stumps. It reaches twenty feet with a four inch trunk diameter. The leaves are five to nine inches long, one and a half to three inches wide, oblong, and pointed with numerous parallel side veins, yellow-green above, paler below, and they turn yellow in the fall. The bark is gray-brown with flat ridges. It blooms in early summer with clusters of white male flowers. There are fewer female flowers and they grow at the base of the male catkins. The burrs are about two to two and a half inches long, and they split in the fall to expose two to three shiny chestnuts which are edible. This tree favors moist soils in mixed

forests from Maine to southwestern Georgia, and Indiana to southern Ontario. It grows in altitudes to 4000 feet.

SWEET CHESTNUT OR SPANISH CHESTNUT
(Castanea vesca [Fagus castanea = Castanea sativa])
A native of southern Europe and western Asia, it attains a gigantic size—trunks can be ten feet in diameter. The nuts are used for cooking. The branches spread widely on every side. The bark is gray and thick with longitudinal furrows, and it twists with age. The leaves are large, glossy, seven to nine inches long, two and a half inches wide, and they turn golden in fall. It flowers in late summer after the leaves have appeared with the male flowers appearing first on catkins. The fruit grows in burrs protected by spines, and it matures in the fall. Frequently found in parks and old estates.

The Horse Chestnut may have derived its name from its ability to cure coughs in horses and cattle. "Horse" may be a corruption of the Welsh "gwres" meaning fierce or hot, whereas the sweet or Spanish Chestnut that is eaten by people is sweet. It must be emphasized again that the Horse Chestnut is not suitable for human consumption, and is in fact not even of the same species as the edible Sweet Chestnut.

One of my favorite personal rituals is the annual harvesting of Horse Chestnuts. When the weather turns cold in September and after a good, hard rain I seek out the trees that I visit each year. Fallen chestnuts are strewn on the grass and sidewalks and some are still in their prickly shells. I put them in plastic bags and freeze them for the winter when I use them to make herbal salves.

 ## Practical Uses

Horse Chestnuts should be soaked in lime water overnight and then boiled for half an hour. After being strained, dried, husked, and ground to a powder, the mixture is nourishing to horses and cattle. One pound of chestnut meal has the equivalent nutrients of seventeen ounces of barley or twenty ounces of hay. Pigs, however, will refuse to eat it. When crushed and simmered in beeswax and oil, Horse Chestnuts make an excellent pain-killing addition to herbal salves.

The Sweet Chestnut, *Castanea vesca,* is named for the town of Castanis in Thessaly where it once flourished. Visitors to Europe will remember this chestnut being cooked in the streets and sold piping hot in France, Germany, Italy, Switzerland, and Spain.

Sweet Chestnut wood loses its durability when the tree is over fifty years old. Young trees are used to make wooden objects that will come into contact with the ground such as fences, stakes, and pilings. The wood has also been used for wine barrels, wood paneling, and in the construction of houses or furniture.

The wood can also be soaked in hot water to leach tannic acid which is then used to tan leather. This process is so effective that Egyptian leather tanned three thousand years ago with Sweet Chestnut tannic acid has been found in good condition.

Sweet Chestnut trees are extremely rare in the United States due to a chestnut blight that has affected most of the country. Large trees are occasionally found, but more often they are the stump sprouts from trees felled long ago. Today, experiments with hybrids are being performed in an attempt to revive these magnificent trees.

Herbal Uses

The bark of the Horse Chestnut can be stripped in the spring and dried in the sun to produce an effective fever remedy. To use it, infuse one ounce of the bark in one pint of water for thirty minutes and take one tablespoon three or four times per day. The tea is also good as a wash for ulcerated skin. (Using only the bark of a branch will protect the tree from harm.)

A tincture of the fruit improves blood circulation and also treats hemorrhoids, rheumatism, and neuralgia. The dose is five to twenty drops, twice a day, in water or herbal tea.

To produce a healing salve for skin irritations, burns, diaper rash, etc., the Horse Chestnut is cracked open with a hammer and simmered for twenty minutes in good quality cold-pressed olive oil. (Use the outer shell as well as the inner meat of the nut.) Heat four tablespoons of beeswax for every cup of oil in a separate pot. Mix the oil and beeswax when they reach the same temperature, strain out the nuts, and place the salve in clean jars. Do not put the lid on until the mixture cools.

The inner skin of the fruit of the Sweet Chestnut may be eaten in small quantities to stop diarrhea. Ground dried nuts mixed with honey make a remedy for coughs and the spitting of blood.

Sweet Chestnut leaves have a sedative affect on the respiratory nerves. Use the leaves either fresh or dried to relieve fevers, paroxysmal, and convulsive coughs (such as whooping cough). Remember that tree leaves are best picked before midsummer due to the gradual buildup of natural insecticides within the plant.

To use the leaves, infuse one ounce of the dried leaves in one pint of just boiled water. The dose is three tablespoons three or four times per day.

Fresh leaves may be pounded to a pulp and mixed with grain alcohol. Bottle and allow to stand for eight days in a cool dark place. The tincture is then filtered. Use the tincture to treat the same conditions that the dried leaves were used for. The dose is five to twenty drops twice per day.

In the homeopathic realm, Horse Chestnut (Aesculus Hippocastanum) is a specific remedy for hemorrhoids and is popular for bowel and liver complaints. The homeopathic preparation of the chestnut leaf (Castanea Vesca) is helpful for whooping cough in its early stages, especially when accompanied by a thirst for warm drinks. Diarrhea and thick urine will also be benefited.

Dr. Bach chose the remedy chestnut bud (from Horse Chestnut) for people who repeatedly make the same mistakes, but seem unable to learn from their experiences. The cause may be indifference, inattention, or failure to anticipate the outcome of their actions. These people try to forget the past, and in the process, lose a grip on the present and future.

When healthy, such individuals are keen observers who gain wisdom from every life experience, and they learn from their own mistakes as well as from the mistakes of others.

The White Chestnut remedy, made from the flowers of Horse Chestnut, helps to prevent recurring negative thoughts. Such people often replay the same "tape" over and over in their mind, thinking of what they "should have said" or "should have done." This mental pattern can weaken the vital life force and result in illness.The condition can become severe and lead to headaches, car accidents, and poor job performance. The individual may wake at night with worries and be unable to sleep, and therefore become fatigued, depressed, and unable to escape from mental torture.

When in a positive state of mind these people have a quiet and serene outlook which is at peace with the world. Their inner thoughts are quiet and create constructive solutions.

Sweet Chestnut was the remedy Bach discovered for despair, and for persons with a hopeless outlook. They are lonely, exhausted, and feel that the future is a void that even death cannot relieve. These people are usually not suicidal, however, and will plod on through sheer strength of will.

The positive aspect of this kind of person is that in the midst of anguish they are still able to put their trust in a higher power. Having experienced the utter desolation of their negative state, they are more than willing to help others in pain and despair.

The Red Chestnut *Aesculus carnea* was used by Dr. Bach to make a flower essence for those who are fearful for others, especially when the anxiety concerns close relations. Over-anxious parents and those who are caring for sick friends and relatives fall into this sphere.

In the positive state, the Red Chestnut person is able to send calm, healing thoughts and courage to those that are near them. Even in states of emergency, they can project assurance to others.

The Native Americans relied on the American Chestnut as a valuable food source. The nuts add carbohydrates, protein, sugar, sulfur, and magnesium to the diet. Chestnuts (other than Horse Chestnuts) can be boiled with brussels sprouts or red cabbage as a vegetable, or they can be cooked in a syrup, pureed, and garnished with whipped cream as a dessert.

To skin the nuts, slit them with a sharp knife and drop them into boiling water for a few minutes. Peel while still warm.

Chestnuts enhance and complement cooked fowl and are often used as a stuffing. To one pound of chestnuts, add one cup of broth, celery, and a pinch of salt, pepper, bay leaf, parsley, and thyme. Cover and simmer for fifteen to twenty minutes. Turn off the heat and add three tablespoons of butter, and a few tablespoons of cream if desired. Serve them hot as a side dish.

The famous French Marons Glacés are made from the Marones Chestnut which is fifteen percent sugar. Chestnut syrup can be refined to make a sugar for home use.

 ## Magical Uses

The chestnut is an herb of Jupiter and of the Fire element. Its primary use in magic is for love spells.

On the slopes of Mount Etna in Sicily, there is a legend surrounding the "Castagno di Cento Cavalli"—the chestnut of a hundred horses—a tree which grew to a circumference of 190 feet. When Jeanne of Aragon paused during her travels to visit Mount Etna, she and her companions were sheltered from a storm under this tree which was large enough to shield the entire company. A house that could hold a shepherd and his flock was later built inside the hollow trunk .

Large trees are a very valuable asset to the physical and mental health of society in general. Tall trees act to conduct energy from the atmosphere to the ground, and vice versa. Large trees in the neighborhood contribute to feelings of stability and strength for the community.

It is always a good idea to develop a relationship with large trees, especially when doing healing work or in times of stress. The trees can safely absorb and ground excess emotional tensions by channeling them deep into the earth.

An old folk tradition states that keeping a chestnut in your pocket or pouch will prevent illnesses that the chestnut is known to cure homeopathically. Considering the minuteness of the homeopathic dose, and the probability that homeopathic remedies may have qualities of nuclear resonance rather than simple materiality, this tradition may have a factual basis. Homeopathic remedies are made by extreme dilution and agitation of alcohol tinctures and they may have no trace of the original substance left. Nuclear resonance tests reveal, however, that these remedies are definitely active on subtle levels.

Oldest of friends, the trees!
Ere fire came, or iron,
Or the shimmering corn:
When the earth mist was dank,
Ere the promise of dawn,
From the slime, from the muck—
The trees!

Nearest of friends, the trees!
They shield us from storm
And brighten our hearths;
They bring to our tables
The autumn's fine gold;
They carol our joys
And sing to our griefs.
They cradle our young
And coffin our dead—
The trees!

Truest of friends, the trees!
Men wander far
At a word or a nod;
Life is a grief,
Love is a chance,
Faith stumbles oft,
Joy is soon past.
Oldest of friends,
Nearest of friends,
Truest of friends,
The trees!
—-Thomas Curtis Clark

Western Red Cedar

Cedar
Fragrant Cedar, Tree of Cleansing Smoke

RED CEDAR *(Juniperus virginiana)*
Native to the United States. It is evergreen and aromatic, and has a compact, columnar crown that may become broad. It grows to sixty feet with a one to two foot trunk diameter. The leaves grow in four rows on slender angled twigs, are scale-like, and dark green. The bark is reddish brown and "shreddy". The cones are berry-like, small, dark blue, juicy, sweet, resinous, and male and female grow on separate trees. This tree favors dry limestone areas and low swampy fields from Maine to northern Florida, and Texas to southern Ontario. It is resistant to cold, heat, and drought.

THE NORTHERN WHITE CEDAR, THE TREE OF LIFE, ARBOR VITAE *(Thuja occidentalis)*
The first native American tree introduced to Europe. Tea made from the foliage and bark saved sailors from scurvy. An aromatic evergreen with a conical crown. It attains a height of seventy feet with a trunk diameter of three feet. The leaves are small, scale-like, in flat pairs with a gland dot, yellow above, and blue-green beneath. The bark is reddish brown and shreddy. The twigs are flattened, jointed, and horizontal. The cones are elliptical, brown, and upright, with eight to ten blunt paired scales. It grows in swamps, in neutral to alkaline soils, from Nova Scotia and Maine, to Illinois and North Carolina. It grows in altitudes to 3000 feet in the southern regions.

Thuja, the Tree of Life, may have received its name when imported to Europe from America in the sixteenth century. Jules Charles de L'Ecluse, a Flemish botanist, named it in 1576, possibly because the tree's structure reminded him of cross sections of the cerebellum of the human brain which has a tree-like form known as the arborvitae.

The French botanist Tournefort probably named Thuja after the Greek thyia or thuia "to fumigate" or thuo "to sacrifice," because of the belief that the ancient Greeks used this tree in their religious rites. The Greeks, however, never specifically identified the special tree that they used.

Cedars were given reverence in biblical scriptures. Solomon discoursed on the virtues of cedar, hyssop, and juniper and commanded that cedar be used in the building of a temple (1 Kings 4:33). In Leviticus 14:4, Moses was commanded by Yaweh to use cedar and hyssop for cleansing. In Ezekiel 31:8 Assyria was compared to a beautiful cedar in God's garden.

Practical Uses

The Red Cedar is best known for its wood which is impervious to weather. This makes cedar an excellent choice for fencing, roofing, shingles, ribs and bottoms of boats, chests, closets, bowls, dishes, and furniture. It is also used in lead pencils, pails, tubs, and boxes for storing furs and woolens. Fresh cedar branches can be made into fragrant and practical brooms.

Cedar, whose oil is an ingredient in natural insect sprays, is an effective insect repellant. An old pillow case filled with cedar chips will keep moths out of your closets. Smaller cedar bundles can be stuffed into nooks and crannies in drawers.

Herbal Uses

Cedar is an example of a plant demonstrating the "Doctrine of Signatures", an ancient concept from a time when few people could read. It was believed that plants bore "signatures" given them by the Creator. With these signatures the herbal virtues of a plant could be discerned. For example, plants useful for liver complaints often have yellow roots or flowers (dandelion, celandine, barberry root). Plants beneficial for the heart are often red (hawthorn, rose hips), and plants that heal mucosa and skin are often mucilaginous (aloe, comfrey). White Cedar grows tiny warts on its leaves and this reveals its healing virtue.

Cedar salves work well for rheumatic afflictions (use fresh leaves to make the salve).

Twigs from this tree can make decoctions which produce herbal abortions. However, they can cause severe gastrointestinal irritation. Small amounts will stimulate the heart muscle and are useful to treat intermittent fevers, rheumatism, oedema, coughs, scurvy, and also work as an emmenagogue (promotes menstruation). Boil one ounce of the twigs in one pint of water. The tea is taken cold, in tablespoon doses, three to six times a day.

To ease severe rheumatic pains, the cones can be dried, powdered, and mixed with oak fern (Polypodium Vulgare) which is best when found growing near or under an oak tree. Mix four parts fern with one part White Cedar cones and add water to give the mixture a pie-dough consistency so it can be applied as a poultice. (Note: the fern roots are generally gathered in the fall.)

An alcohol tincture of White Cedar is known for its effect on venereal warts (condylomata) and it can remove them completely in three or four weeks. The tincture is taken internally or applied locally to the affected area. To make the tincture, take fresh branchlets, leaves, and flowers, pound them to a pulp (or use a blender) and add two-thirds of their weight in grain alcohol. Store for eight days in a cool, dark place—then strain, filter, and store in dark glass bottles. The dose is five to twenty drops, three times per day.

In homeopathy, White Cedar's (Thuja Occidentalis) main sphere of action is the genito-urinary tract where it has an anti-bacterial affect. Gonorrhea, variola, warty excrescences and complaints resulting from the aftereffects of vaccination have all been relieved by White Cedar. It is sometimes used to treat asthma in children.

Native Americans made a decoction of the inner bark of the tree to treat headaches, heart pain, to "bring down" the menses, and to relieve swellings.

The leaf or the oil of the leaf is used to scent soap. Caution: the oil should never be ingested as it can be extremely toxic, even fatal.

The fresh leaf of Red Cedar is also used for salves. The ointment made from it is an irritant which promotes a discharge from blisters. The tea of the leaf is diuretic.

Red Cedar berries are used in decoctions to promote sweating and induce menstruation. "Cedar apples," or "warts" found on the branches, are used to make a worming medicine. They are dried, powdered and taken internally in capsules. The dose is ten to twenty grains, three times per day. Red

Cedar oil is applied locally for arthritic and rheumatic pain. It is also used to scent soaps. Native Americans inhaled smoke from burning Red Cedar wood and leaves to relieve chest colds and flu.

Magical Uses

Cedar is one of the "Nine Sacred Woods" suitable for all magical workings and earth rituals. Cedar is an herb of the sun, its element is Fire, and it is especially effective for burning at Yule and during winter rites. It is sacred to Astarte and to Wotan. Cedar bestows qualities of prosperity, protection, and healing. If cedar is unavailable, juniper can be used as a substitute.

The Old Testament refers to cedar as a tree used by Solomon to build his temple. In the ancient world, wise and spiritual people were sometimes compared to trees. Some say that the "Cedars of Lebanon" referred to people rather than trees. When Palestine was once covered with forests, the cedar forest at Elam was considered very sacred.

Maskims, ancient Chaldean spirits, were kept at bay with White Cedar which was considered effective to protect people and places from spells and evil influences.

An ancient Babylonian magical text describes how a man possessed with seven evil spirits can be rid of them. First, he must go to a cedar tree, which shatters the power of the incubus. Then, with the help of an amulet placed on the sick man's head, he must invoke the aid of the Fire God to dispel the demons.

Another text describes the initiation of a seer. At one point the initiate descends through meditation to the lower world where he sees altars in the waters, tablets of the Gods, and the divine cedar tree which is beloved to the Gods.

Cedar was the World Tree, the essence of life and renewal. These trees appear frequently on Assyrian sculptures and tablets. Often the number seven is incorporated in the depictions, with four branches on one side of the trunk and three on the other.

Japanese tradition believes that trees have souls. Old Japanese legends speak of ancient cedars that oozed blood when cut by an axe.

In China, cedars are known as the "Trees of Faithful Love." According to an old legend, Hanpang was a secretary to King Kang of the Sung dynasty. Hanpang and his wife loved each other dearly, but the King lusted after his wife, Ho, and had Hanpang thrown in jail, where he died of grief. On learning of her husband's death, Ho leapt from a high terrace to escape the King's passions. Her clothing contained a last request asking that she be buried with her beloved husband. Angry, the King refused to honor her wishes and ordered that the couple be buried apart. During the night, however, Heaven's true will was revealed—two cedars grew from the two graves and within ten days their branches and roots were joined.

As an incense, cedar purifies an area and banishes nightmares. Native Americans sometimes burn cedar in sweat lodges to help release heavy emotional energies. Cedar incense is also effective at child blessings and naming ceremonies.

Hung in the house, cedar repels lightning and protects the home from negative energies of all kinds. Place cedar in your wallet or pouch to attract money, or burn it to attract financial success and increase psychic powers. Add it to love charms.

To burn cedar, use the sawdust or grind the dried leaves and burn them on charcoal bricks. Native Americans made "smudge sticks" for the purification and consecration of a ritual space and its celebrants. To make a smudge stick, simply lay sprigs of cedar in a vertical pile in the center of several sheets of newspaper. Keep all the stems pointing in one direction and place sage in the center. Other herbs such as vervain, mugwort, spearmint, etc., may be added if desired to achieve varying psychic effects. Roll up the newspaper into a "cigar" shaped package and tie it securely with string. After three or four months of drying, unwrap the bundle and the sticks will be perfectly formed.

The sticks can then be tied with strings of various colors (these colors symbolize specific energies) and decorated with feathers on the holding end (where the stems are). It is now ready for ritual use.

Cedar smoke can be used to consecrate wands and it is said to complement the study of the Wands suit in the Tarot deck. Amethysts and sapphires have a special affinity with cedar and these gems should be stored in a cedar box.

Quaking Aspen

Poplar
Trembling Poplar, Tree that Transcends Fear

BALSAM POPLAR, TACAMAHAC, BALM OF GILEAD
(Populus balsamifera = Populus candicans)
The most northern American hardwood. A large tree with a nar-
row, open crown, and resinous, fragrant buds. It grows to ninety
feet with a trunk diameter of three feet. The leaves are three to
five inches long, one and a half to three inches wide, ovate,
pointed with a rounded base, wavy toothed, dark green above,
and whitish beneath. The bark is light brown and smooth, and
becomes gray and furrowed with age. The buds are fragrant
with a yellow resin that smells like balsam. The male and
female catkins flower on separate trees in the spring. The egg
shaped capsules mature in spring and split releasing cottony
seeds. This tree favors moist valleys, stream banks, and flood
plains. Its range is from Labrador to Alaska, and south from
Pennsylvania and West Virginia to Colorado. It grows in al-
titudes to 5500 feet.

BLACK POPLAR, LOMBARDY POPLAR *(Populus nigra)*
Originally from Europe and western Asia, it was cultivated in
Italy before 1750. It is fast growing but very short lived. It has a
straight trunk and a narrow, columnar crown. It grows to sixty
feet and has a trunk diameter of two feet. The leaves are one
and a half to three inches long, triangular, long pointed, wavy,
saw-toothed, and paler beneath. The bark is gray and deeply
furrowed. The twigs are orange and become gray later in life.
The catkins appear in early spring before the leaves have
developed, are two inches long, and drooping. This tree favors
moist soil in temperate areas. Common across the United
States.

TREMBLING ASPEN, QUAKING ASPEN, AMERICAN ASPEN
(Populus tremuloides)
A native tree across America, it is the first to appear after a
forest fire. It attains a height of seventy feet with a trunk
diameter of one and a half feet. The leaves are one and a
quarter to three inches long, nearly round, short-pointed, and

finely toothed. The leaves are golden yellow in the fall. The bark is smooth and whitish and becomes gray and furrowed with age. The male and female catkins appear on separate trees before the leaves in early spring. The fruit is a conical, green capsule that splits in late spring to release cottony seeds (in the west propagation is mostly by root sprouts). This tree favors sandy and gravelly soil below spruce forests. Its range is from Newfoundland to Alaska, and from Virginia to northern Mexico. It grows in altitudes to 10,000 feet. It is easily broken by storms.

Poplar is the sacred World Tree of the Lakota nation. For the sun dance ceremony, a poplar is carefully cut and lowered to be re-erected in the center of the dance circle. While being carried it must never touch the ground. Green branches, a buffalo skull, and eagle feathers adorn the tree during the rite.

Practical Uses

The wood of the poplar tree is light and is used to make household utensils. In the early spring, the Cree Indians of North America ate the inner bark, which they called "Metoos," as an emergency food. The leaves and young shoots are used in Sweden as sheep fodder, and in Europe the inner bark was used to make bread during times of famine.

It was fascinating to discover that the Black Poplar was a funeral tree in ancient Greece, regarded as sacred to the Earth Mother, while in old Ireland the "fe" or measuring rod used by coffin makers to measure corpses was made of poplar wood. Mesopotamian graves of 3000 B.C. were found to contain golden headdresses of poplar.

The leaves of the Lombardy Poplar are used to impart a lime-yellow color to alum mordanted wool and will turn wool and chrome golden brown.

Herbal Uses

Poplar is similar to willow in its therapeutic use and is considered superior for the treatment of intermittent fevers such as malaria. Like the willow, it is rich in salicin—the

chemical basis for our modern drug aspirin. Old homeopaths
and pharmacists made an alcohol tincture of the fresh inner
bark of Quaking Aspen (Populus Tremuloides) with which
they treated fever, jaundice, and worms.

Quaking Aspen, or White Poplar, is used to treat fevers,
urinary infections, kidney weakness, gonorrhea, uterine
problems, chronic diarrhea, diabetes, hay fever, and "gleet"
(an aftereffect of venereal diseases that results in a constant
discharge). It is relaxing to the intestines and relieves
headaches caused by liver congestion.

Soak the buds of the tree in alcohol and then make a
decoction (adding the alcohol to the brew), or simmer one
teaspoon of leaf, buds, or bark in one cup of water. The dose
is one or two cups a day.

Tea made of poplar bark is good for coughs and excellent
as a gargle for sore throats. The tea can also be used externally
as a wash for inflammations, cuts, wounds, and burns. A salve
can be produced by boiling the buds in olive oil and adding
four tablespoons of melted beeswax for each cup of oil. (The
oil and beeswax must be the same temperature when mixed or
they won't blend properly.)

Populus candicans, or "Balm of Gilead," is used in much
the same way. The resinous buds are boiled in water to create
a remedy rich in vitamin C which is a stimulating tonic for lung,
stomach, and kidney conditions. Because of the salicin it contains, it will also help ease rheumatic pains. A salve made with
the buds, olive oil, and beeswax will help heal bruises, swellings, and skin conditions.

The tincture made from the bud of the Balm of Gilead
(Populus Candicans) is used homeopathically to treat acute
colds, especially when they are accompanied by loss of voice or
hoarseness.

Balsam Poplar can also provide an effective tea or salve. It
is a more northern tree that is also very high in vitamin C.
Simmer the buds for lung congestion. Tinctured, they will help
stomach, lung, and kidney problems as well as rheumatic complaints.

Black Poplar leaves are crushed with vinegar and applied
as a poultice for gout. This tree's buds are made into an ointment for hemorrhoids, arthritis, and rheumatism. To heal
bronchitis, the salve may be rubbed directly on the chest.

The Lombardy Poplar, a fast growing species from Italy, is

also useful to heal wounds. Simmer the leaf buds to make a beeswax and oil salve.

American Aspen is used for cystitis, night sweats, nausea, vomiting, painful urination, and malarial fevers. Collect the bark in the spring and use it in a tincture or a standard decoction.

Dr. Edward Bach saw in the Quaking Aspen the picture of an anxiety ridden person plagued with vague worries about unknown things. These people awaken from sleep in sudden terror and have a great fear of recurring nightmares. They may fear death or have a religious mania. The sense of panic can appear suddenly whether the person is alone or with company. The fear can strike so deep it can produce trembling and sweating. The remedy for these people is the aspen flower essence which is made by sun potentization of the buds and flowers.

The positive aspect of the aspen type is their fearless certainty that unconditional love is at the very foundation of the universe. They can possess an intuitive and joy-filled understanding that death is an illusion and have a sense that life is a never-ending adventure.

Magical Uses

It was once believed that humans originated from trees. Classical mythology contains many stories of individuals transformed into trees.

One myth speaks of Phoeton, son of Helios, the Sun God. Because Epaphus, a son of Zeus, and Io disputed Phoeton's parentage, Phoeton begged Helios to grant him a wish to prove his paternity. Helios declared that he would not refuse Phoeton's wish. Phoeton then asked to drive the chariot of the sun for a day, an important request which astounded Helios. Helios tried in vain to dissuade Phoeton from his demand, but, bound by his oath, he could not refuse.

Phoeton, inexperienced and weak, lost control of the horses and chariot. As a result the sun came so close to the earth that water dried up, the earth caught fire, and the rivers began to boil.

Zeus, in his anger at the destruction of earth and sky, slew Phoeton with a lightning bolt and threw him into the river

Eridanus. Phoeton's sisters, the Heliades, wept in their grief and were transformed into poplars. Their tears were said to turn to amber (elektron) as they dropped into the river.

In another myth, Pluto/Hades, Lord of the Underworld, loved O'keanis Leuke. At her death he caused the White Poplar to appear on the Elysian plain.

The poplar is of the Water element and is a herb of Saturn. It is a suitable wood to burn in ritual fires and for magical workings.

Place the buds and leaves in sachets to attract money or burn them as incense to create financial security. The buds are sometimes added to flying ointments.

Ancient shield makers used poplar. They believed its wood offered protection from death and disease. They felt that its trembling leaves were having discourse with the wind, the "messenger of the Gods." Poplar wood brought protection and endurance, and it also helped the aspirant to hear the guidance of the spirit as it moved within and without.

Western Larch

Larch

Larch, Tree of Sanctity

WESTERN LARCH, MONTANA LARCH, WESTERN TAMARACK
(Larix occidentalis)
*A tall, deciduous tree with a pyramidal head that grows to a
height of 150 feet. The bark is dark and becomes cinnamon red
on older trees. It has short, horizontal branches with rigid
leaves, sharply pointed, triangular and keeled beneath. The
leaves are one to one and three quarter inches long and pale
green. The cones are oblong, one and a half inches long. Its
bracts are larger than its scales which are numerous, stiff,
spreading or recurved after maturity. The branchlets are pubes-
cent when young. It is found from British Columbia to Oregon
and Montana, seldom below 2000 feet or above 7000 feet. The
greatest size and abundance of these trees is in Montana.*

EUROPEAN LARCH *(Larix decidua = Pinus larix =
L. europea)*
*A native of northern and central Europe, it is the source of
Venetian turpentine, a medicinal resin. A deciduous tree with
an open, pyramidal crown that becomes irregular with age. It
grows to seventy feet with a trunk diameter of two feet. The
needles are light green and turn yellow before dropping off in
the fall. They are about one inch long, soft and flattened,
with thirty to forty growing on a twig. The bark is gray to
brown, thick, scaly, and furrowed. The cones are up to one
and a quarter inches long, upright and ovoid, reddish when
immature, and turning gray with age. This tree favors moist,
cool regions and high altitudes. Common in the northeastern
United States, especially in parks and gardens, and in the
midwest.*

A magnificent larch tree grows on the campus of Amherst
College in Amherst, Massachusetts. It towers over the surrounding oaks and maples which are of considerable age. It is
easy to see why the ancient tribes of the Russian woodlands
venerated this tree. The larch was the Siberian World Tree on

which the sun and moon ascended and descended in the forms of golden and silver birds.

Practical Uses

Larch is grown in the United States primarily as an ornamental. A member of the pine family, it grows six times faster than oak. Of all the conifers, larch has the strongest and most durable wood and it has been used for mining operations and railway ties. It is also suitable for ship building, house construction, and cabinet making. Naturally resistant to fungus and worms, larch wood is a good choice for picture backings and frames. Larch bark has been used for tanning although oak is more effective.

Because the larch drops its needles in the autumn, unlike other conifers, it tends to improve the quality and quantity of the surrounding earth.

Pagan peoples of northern Europe had high regard for the larch. Sacred groves in northern areas were often planted with larches. The larch is a tree of spiritual expression. The larch is a deciduous conifer which retains the familiar round and pointed structure of conifers in general.

Herbal Uses

A cold decoction of the inner bark of larch is administered as a diuretic in cases of water retention and oedema. The powdered bark can be applied as a poultice on difficult wounds. The inner bark is gently stimulating to a sluggish, hardened liver and spleen, and relieves melancholy. Use larch for chronic bleeding of the lungs, bowels, or stomach, and for excessive menstruation. Steep one teaspoon of the inner bark in one cup of boiling water for thirty minutes.

The needles and shoots of larch are simmered in a large pot and strained to make a stimulating bath additive.

The sap or resin, which is strained for medicines and varnishes, is collected from May to October. The best time to collect tree sap is during the time of the full moon. Tree sap reacts to the phases of the moon and the wood will contain more sap near the full moon. The resins of conifers can be applied to wounded trees for healing and the same resins seem to have antiseptic and healing effects on human injuries.

The European Larch and the Western Larch (Larix Occidentalis) are tapped for their resin known as "venice turpentine." The resin may be used as it comes from the tree after careful filtering with gauze. Five to eight drops are taken with honey to expel tapeworms, treat bloody diarrhea, and to encourage menstruation. The resin is useful as a stimulating expectorant in bronchitis, to stop internal hemorrhages, and to heal cystitis.

Apply the resin externally to wounds and sores by placing five drops in a bowl of water and soaking a cloth in the mixture. Place the cloth on the affected part, once a day, for thirty minutes and no more.

Caution: use only a few drops for internal or external application as large amounts of resin can cause kidney damage or blistering on the skin.

Use the fomentation for eczema and psoriasis. It has also been used as a disinfectant on gangrenous tissue.

Dr. Edward Bach chose larch as the flower essence for those who lack self confidence. Such people don't even attempt to succeed because they are convinced they will fail. This insecurity arises not from fear, but rather from a poor self image. Ironically, this type is often quite capable, though they never give themselves a chance, often resulting in a lack of determination which can lead to feelings of great despair. Such individuals will genuinely admire the abilities of others and be firmly convinced that they lack those admirable qualities within themselves.

When healthy, these people are willing to take risks and give life their best.

Magical Uses

The Turanian tribes of Siberia chose groves of larches for their spring rites during which they offered horses and oxen in sacrifice to the Spirit of the Forest. Idols dressed in fur were set beneath trees whose trunks were wrapped in cloth or tin. Reindeer hides, pelts, pots, spoons, snuff boxes, and other household items were left as offerings to the gods.

The act of offering sacrifices is a difficult concept for

modern folk to appreciate. Keep in mind that these people had a deep and genuine feeling for the gifts the forest had bestowed on them. They were conscious of the many lives that were sacrificed, both plant and animal, to ensure the survival of their clans. Because they felt the need for a balanced existence with all life, an attempt was made to repay some of the wealth that Nature had bestowed on them.

To the Ostyacks of Siberia, seven larch trees constituted a sacred grove. Anyone passing by would leave an arrow or hang a fur from the trees. Hunting, fishing, and the drinking of water were forbidden in a sacred grove. It was believed that cutting down a tree, or even breaking a twig, could result in death for the offender.

In Russia, rainmakers worked in sacred groves of larch. Three men would climb a tree. One would bang on a kettle to imitate the sound of thunder, another would strike two burning sticks together to make sparks fly like lightning. The third would use a bundle of twigs to sprinkle water from a pot.

A sacred larch tree stood at Nauders in the Tyrol, Austria until 1859. According to legend, it was said that if the tree was cut in any way it would bleed and the person guilty of the injury would also be wounded. The offender would only be healed after the tree's scar had filled over. Arguing and swearing were forbidden near the tree because the surrounding ground was considered holy.

Larch can be worn as a protection from negative influences or placed in sachets to prevent fires.

You come to fetch me from my work tonight
When supper's on the table, and we'll see
If I can leave off burying the white
Soft petals fallen from the apple tree
(Soft petals, yes, but not so barren quite,
Mingled with these, smooth bean and wrinkled pea;)
And go along with you ere you lose sight
Of what you came for and become like me,
Slave to a springtime passion for the earth.
How Love burns through the Putting in the Seed
On through the watching for that early birth
When, just as the soil tarnishes with weed,
The sturdy seedling with arched body comes
Shouldering its way and shedding the earth crumbs.
—Robert Frost

Black Walnut

Walnut
Walnut, the Spell Breaker

BUTTERNUT, WHITE WALNUT *(Juglans cinerea)*
The nuts are edible. The tree has a short trunk, thick branches, and a wide, open crown. It attains a height of ninety feet with a trunk diameter of two feet. The leaves are pinnately compound, fifteen to twenty-four inches long, have eleven to seventeen leaflets, are up to four and a half inches long, broadly lanceolate, pointed at the tip, rounded at the base, finely saw-toothed, paler beneath, and yellow or brown in the fall. The bark is light gray and becomes rough and furrowed with age. The male flowers are small, greenish catkins. The female flower has two lobe shaped styles, and blooms in early spring. The fruit is up to two and a half inches long, egg shaped, and grows in drooping clusters of three to five. The shell of the nut is light brown, rough and ridged, and contains the edible nut. This tree favors moist valleys and the dry rocky soil of hardwood forests. Its range is from New Brunswick to northern Georgia, and from Arkansas to Minnesota and Quebec. It grows in altitudes to 4800 feet.

BLACK WALNUT, AMERICAN WALNUT *(Juglans nigra)*
An American native with edible nuts and roots that are toxic to many plants. A large tree that can reach 150 feet with a trunk diameter of four feet. The leaves are pinnately compound, twelve to twenty-four inches long with up to twenty-one leaflets, are two and a half to five inches long, broadly lanceolate, finely saw-toothed, and turn yellow in the fall. The bark is dark brown and deeply furrowed. This tree blooms in early spring with the male catkins and female flowers growing at the tip of the same twig. The fruit may be paired or single, are up to two and a half inches in diameter with a brown or green husk that is ridged and thick and covers the edible seed. The tree favors moist soils and mixed forests. Its range is from New York to northwest Florida, and from Texas to southern Ontario and New England. It grows in altitudes to 4000 feet.

ENGLISH WALNUT *(Juglans regia)*
The bark and leaves are used internally and externally as
medicine. A native of Europe and China. It grows to ninety feet
with a spreading crown and a massive stem. The leaves are
deciduous and pinnate. The bark is silver gray. The flowers of
both sexes appear before the leaves and grow together on the
same tree. The green husks make a yellow dye. Frequently in-
jured by spring frosts, this tree is cultivated mainly in Califor-
nia, but is also successful as far north as Boston.

Walnut trees originated in Lebanon, Kashmir, Kumdon, Sirmore, Nepal, and the Himalayas. Pliny, a Roman naturalist, encyclopedist, and writer, tells us that they were brought to Italy by the Persians. By 150 B.C. they were well established and spread throughout Europe. There is a legend that in the Golden Age humans lived on acorns but the Gods lived on walnuts, hence the latin Juglans from "Jovis glans" or "Jupiter's nuts."

The name "walnut" is from the Teutonic "welsche nuss" or "foreign nut."

The fall equinox is the time to perform the yearly ritual of gathering walnuts in their green hulls. The fresh green rinds are peeled and added to healing salves.

 ## Practical Uses

Walnut wood is excellent for furniture, gunstocks, and inlays. In the past, the wheels and bodies of coaches were fashioned out of walnut. It is not a good choice for buildings, however, as the wood becomes quite brittle with age.

The oil of the kernel is applied as a wood polish and mixed with varnishes and stains. In woodwork, the nut produces a dark stain.

Walnut oil is a delicious addition to salads, or it can be used for frying and other culinary processes. Fifteen pounds of kernels produce seven pounds of oil. In France it was once used as a lamp oil.

The husks and leaves of the walnut may be infused in boiled water, cooled, and poured on plants that are plagued by worms or other insect pests.

The green hulls of the Black Walnut will produce a dark

brown color in wool, with or without alum mordanting. Adding chrome to the wool results in a light brown color. Copperas brings out a medium brown, and tin a darker brown. The green Husks of the English Walnut make a yellow dye.

Herbal Uses

The green outer covering of the nut resembles the pericranium of the skull and, according to the Doctrine of Signatures, this reveals its effectiveness in the treatment of head wounds. The inner nut is similar to the skull as its yellow skin stretches over the kernel like the meninges tissue covers the brain. The kernel resembles the brain itself and traditional herbalists made a poultice of walnuts and wine which they applied to the head to relieve pain.

The Eclectic School of Medicine, which flourished in the nineteenth century, listed walnuts as a source of one of the most important skin remedies. A salve will be useful for skin irritations, burns, dry eczema, and flesh wounds (use the green husks of the nut to make the salve). Be sure to wear rubber gloves when you cut up the husks as the dark stain will remain on your hands for weeks.

Traditional herbalists relied on walnut as a slow, but effective, treatment for intestinal diseases and inflammations, syphilis, tapeworm, cancer, scrofula, ulcers, boils, skin irritations, eye problems, and liver complaints. It was also considered helpful for hemorrhoids, prolapsed uterus or intestines, varicose veins, mucus and hemorrhagic discharges, leucorrhea, diarrhea, dysentery, sore throats, tonsillitis, nasal catarrh, hair loss, and to dry up breast milk.

Boil the green husks with honey and water to make a sore throat gargle. The husk, shell, and peel of the unripe walnut are simmered for ten to twenty minutes and taken hot to promote sweating and to lower the temperature of fevers. The dosage is about one ounce of the mixture to a pint of water, or about two teaspoons per cup. The decoction of the green shell of the English Walnut has been used as a remedy for failing virility. For this purpose, four teaspoons of the leaf or the chopped green husk are simmered in one cup of water. The dose is one cup per day in small doses.

The green unripe husks are antiseptic, germicidal, vermicidal, and a parasiticide. The resulting brown stain is like an organic iodine. A piece of the husk may be inserted into a hollow tooth to ease pain until treatment by a dentist can be obtained.

Gather the leaves in late spring or early summer and dry them carefully. The best time to gather them is on a sunny morning after the dew has evaporated. The leaves are dried either indoors or outside in the shade. Once dried, the leaves are powdered and applied directly to moist skin conditions and bleeding surfaces. A wide acting remedy can be made by steeping two ounces of the cut or powdered leaf in one and a half pints of boiled water for fifteen minutes. Strain and sweeten if necessary. The adult dose is one quarter cup four times per day.

The English Walnut is used as a bath additive made by boiling one pound of the dried leaf in one and a half quarts of water for forty-five minutes and straining the liquid into the bath.

Walnut flour is commonly added to fruit cakes and nut breads. Walnuts are a good source of manganese, a dietary nutrient known to benefit conditions such as schizophrenia.

The tea from the leaves is a tonic for the stomach, an appetite stimulant, an external wash for glandular swellings and skin problems, and is used to dry up breast milk. The same formula (minus the sweeteners) is appropriate for external applications. For skin conditions, soak a clean cotton cloth in the infusion and apply. Leave it on until it dries. The infusion is a good gargle for sore throats and a mouth wash for mouth sores. For this purpose it is taken three times per day. For catarrh of the nasal passages, use the infusion as a spray, or insert into the nose with a cotton ball or a swab. For scalp problems such as itch, dandruff, or falling hair, apply the infusion as a lotion twice per day, using no soap, and washing the hair with hot water only.

For enemas and douches, one pint of the infusion is injected full strength. Dilute the tea with three times its volume of water when treating a child. The enema should be repeated every three or four hours and the douche twice per day. These methods are known to benefit hemorrhoids, diarrhea, and vaginitis.

The bark of the root is the most medicinally active part of the walnut tree. Tinctures can be made of it and taken in doses of fifteen drops.

Steep one ounce of the dried bark in one pint of boiled water for six hours and strain. For a laxative or purgative, drink one quarter cup three times per day. External ulcers can be healed by washing the affected areas with the above formula that is mixed with a small amount of sugar. The infusion or decoction of the bark may be used to treat diarrhea and to stop milk flow.

The thin, yellow membrane that covers the inner nut is dried and powdered and used as a remedy for colic when mixed with peppermint tea and given in teaspoon doses.

The Butternut provides a remedy for worms, fevers, colds, flu, and chronic constipation. To make a medicinal syrup, boil one pound of bark in one quart of water until it evaporates down to one pint. Add one pound sugar and boil to a syrup consistency. The dose is one teaspoon several times a day. Butternut is also used for occipital headaches associated with jaundice and skin eruptions.

Native Americans used the oil of the nuts extensively. A primary use was to anoint heads during ceremonies.

In the homeopathic realm, the English Walnut (Juglans Regia) is used principally for skin eruptions, acne, sharp pains in the occipital region, and sties.

Dr. Edward Bach called walnut the "link breaker," the great remedy for the transitional phases of life. Individuals benefited by the walnut are guided by unconventional ideals and ambitions, and are not easily influenced by others. These people have a mission to fulfill and it is important that they not be held back by the past. Old habits and family ties are seen as obstacles that frustrate their plans.

Walnut is used to free an individual in times of transition such as puberty, menopause, teething, etc. Changes of religion, a move to a new area of the country, or any step that requires the breaking of old limits, habits, and associations will be eased by this remedy. Dr. Bach called walnut the "great spell breaker" of heredity, the past, and of the present environment.

In their positive aspect, these people display certitude and a determination to carry out their beliefs. They perform their life's work with no concern for the opinion of others. These people are the ones who fearlessly bring new ideas to their society and their world.

Walnut Pickle

Select green, unripe walnuts that are soft enough to be pierced with a skewer or knitting needle. Pour boiling water over them and rub until any external fuzz comes off. Cover with water and boil until the water becomes quite dark. Pour the water off and repeat the process until the water remains clear. Place the walnuts in a jar with salt, ginger, black pepper, bay leaf, mustard seed, horseradish, lemon slices, cloves, mace, and a few walnut leaves. Pour boiling vinegar over the whole and seal. Allow to stand for at least thirty days. The strained vinegar makes a good sore throat gargle.

Walnuts in Syrup

Test green walnuts to see if a needle pierces them easily (about mid-July). Soak in water for nine days, washing them morning and evening. Then boil in water until soft. Drain and pierce each nut with a skewer and insert a clove into the hole. Add cinnamon, lemon peel, and sugar equal to the weight of the nuts. Boil the nuts until tender, and drain, removing the thin, green skin with a cloth. The finished nuts are said to help digestion.

A note about sugar: Sugar has been mentioned several times in this chapter as an addition to recipes and skin preparations. The best sugar that I am aware of is "Sucanat" which is brown, unrefined sugar made from evaporated organic sugar-cane juice. Unlike white sugar, this sugar does not cause cavities and it actually has nutritional value. One teaspoon provides 33 International Units of vitamin A, one mg. of vitamin C, traces of B1, B2, B6, and niacin, about three mg. of calcium, thirteen mg. of iron, one mg. of phosphorus, about two and a half mg. of magnesium and traces of zinc, copper, and pantothenic acid. In contrast, white sugar provides only empty calories and damages the teeth and body metabolism.

Magical Use

The walnut tree is a tree of the sun, and it is of the Fire element. Its qualities are love, fertility, healing, and mental acuity. The town of Bethlehem was once the location of a grove sacred to the god Adonis.

In ancient Phoenicia, Byblos was the center of worship for

Adonis. Near there, on the slopes of Mount Lebanon in Aphaca, a grove and sanctuary of Astarte (another name for the Goddess Aphrodite/Venus) existed where walnuts grow to this day. Legend states that here Adonis met Aphrodite and was killed by a wild boar.

Aphrodite's grief was so acute that she held onto his body until the gods declared that her lover would be allowed to live on earth during the spring and summer, and that she could spend the other half of the year with him in the underworld. (Aphrodite is the goddess of flowers and gardens.) The festival of Adonis is celebrated by first mourning his death and then raising the shout "Adonis lives and is risen again!"

The King of Laconia, Dion, was once privileged to give hospitality to the god, Apollo. As a reward, his three daughters were given the gift of prophecy on the condition that it be used wisely and never to pry into other people's business unbidden.

Carya, the youngest of the sisters was the beloved of the God Bacchus, for which she was envied by her sisters who proceeded to become quite jealous. When Carya misused the gift of prophesy, thereby breaking the sisters' promise, Apollo, as a punishment, transformed the jealous sisters into stones, but changed Carya into a walnut tree. Perceiving that she had been saved from the wrath of the gods by her loving nature, traditional wisdom has associated the walnut with the powers of love ever since.

Legend states that witches once danced beneath a walnut tree growing in Benevento, Italy. According to another medieval legend, many pagan rituals were performed beneath this tree. It is no surprise that such a tree would be so honored considering the healing properties of the walnut, and the healing role of witches. Although Barbatus, a Christian saint, had the tree cut down in an effort to halt the pagan proceedings, whenever the witches danced at that spot a new walnut tree appeared.

Carry the nuts to enhance fertility, strengthen the heart, and protect against rheumatism. Eating walnuts may help to cure madness. Wearing walnut leaves either as a crown, or around a hat, can prevent headache and sunstroke. If you receive a gift of walnuts, your wishes will come true. A bride who desires to postpone childbearing should wear in her bodice as many roasted walnuts as years she wishes to avoid childbirth.

Common Elder

Elder

Elder Mother, Compassionate Forest Spirit

DWARF ELDER *(Sambucus ebulus)*
*A perennial shrub, it grows in eastern and central United States
and in Europe. The root stock produces erect, grooved stems
with odd, pinnate leaves. The leaflets are lanceolate and ser-
rated. White flowers with a reddish purple tinge appear from
June to August. The fruit is black and shiny with four seeds and
poisonous.*

ELDERBERRY, COMMON ELDER, AMERICAN ELDER
(Sambucus canadensis = Sambucus nigra)
*A perennial shrub with an irregular crown and spreading
branches. It attains a height of sixteen feet with a trunk
diameter of six inches. The leaves are opposite, pinnately compound, five to nine inches long, with three to seven leaflets, elliptical, in pairs, and saw-toothed. The leaves are shiny green
above and dull beneath. The bark is light gray or brown with
raised dots and it becomes rough with age. The twigs have
ringed nodes and a thick pale pith. The white flowers are a
quarter of an inch wide, fragrant, and grow in flat-topped
clusters that are four to eight inches wide. They bloom in early
summer. The berries are black or deep maroon-purple, juicy,
somewhat sweet, and they appear in late summer. This tree
favors streams and wet soils from Nova Scotia to southern
Florida, and from Texas to southeastern Manitoba. It grows in
altitudes to 5000 feet.*

I never feel the presence of the ancient foremothers so
strongly as when the elder blooms. When describing the tree I
am tempted to call it "her." The spirit of this tree is of the all
powerful, all healing, Great Mother. To this day in parts of
England, Ireland, Scotland, and Wales it is considered a grave
wrong to burn her wood. The many prohibitions surrounding
the harming of an elder tree may stem from her great useful-
ness in medicine and in magic.

Grieve's Herbal gives the most thorough introduction to

the uses and lore of this plant. Every part of the tree has healing virtues—from the bark of the root to the delicate white flowers and berries.

The word elder comes to us from the Anglo-Saxon "aeld," fire, because hollowed elder branches were once used to kindle fires by blowing through them. The elder is also known as "Pipe-tree" since the pith can be easily removed to make hollow pipes and flutes. According to Grieve, *Sambucus,* the generic name, may be derived from the Greek sambuca, "sackbut," the name of an ancient stringed instrument used in Greece and the Middle East. More likely it may have evolved from a pipe called "sampogna" fashioned by Italian peasants.

In Sicily, an elder branch is considered the best wood for repelling robbers and snakes.

Practical Uses

Elder wood is white, close grained, and polishes easily. It was once used to make skewers, pegs, parts of fishing rods, needles for net weaving, combs, and to construct mathematical, scientific, and musical instruments. Elder wood was used in garden fences for it was said to last longer in the ground than an iron bar. The inner pith was used in experiments with electricity and for making toys.

The leaves are decocted to make a natural insecticide that repels aphids and caterpillars. To fend off flies, elder leaves can be crushed and rubbed on the face or one's hat. An infusion of fresh leaves is a mosquito and gnat repellent when worn on the skin, and also repels mice and moles when poured into their holes.

The young shoots are boiled to prepare a remedy for blight in fruit trees. (Other ingredients that should be added to the mix for the prevention and cure of fruit blight include copper sulphate, iron sulphate, nicotine, soft soap, methylated spirit, and slaked lime.)

The bark and roots yield a black dye for wool while the leaves with alum make green. The berries will dye articles purple or blue, and the juice with alum makes a violet color. Alum and salt added to the berries creates a lilac color.

Sheep and cows are fond of the greens. Sheep affected with foot-rot may be cured by eating the bark and shoots.

Elderberries, however, are dangerous to chickens and the flowers can be fatal to turkeys.

The bark, leaves, flowers, and berries of the Elderberry are used in medicine.

The ancient Romans boiled the berries in wine to dye their hair black, or at least a deep purple.

Herbal Uses

The elder is truly a universal remedy since all its parts can be used, in every possible form, to treat seventy or more conditions.

The berries are completely safe for people when eaten ripe. They are used to make teas, wines, preserves, and baked goods. Elderberry wine is tasty and is also a remedy for rheumatic pains and neuralgia.

The leaves and flowers of the elder are incorporated into drinks, poultices, and salves. Elder vinegar complements salads. Even a fungus *Hirneola auricula-judae* growing on the trees in shady, damp areas has been jellied and used for mouth, throat, and uvular inflammations.

The bark of the root is used fresh for headaches, mucus congestion, to promote labor, and as a poultice for mastitis. The inner bark of the elder is best gathered from young trees in the fall and dried in the sun. At night it should be brought indoors to avoid contamination from dampness.

The bark is purgative and in large doses results in vomiting. In smaller doses it is mainly used as a diuretic for edematous conditions connected with kidney and heart problems. The usual method of preparation is to infuse one ounce of bark in one pint of boiled water for about forty-five minutes. The dose is a quarter cup. (Please see a health professional before using diuretics.) The green inner bark is also used in salves.

The leaves may be used fresh or dry. Collect them on a clear day in early summer or late spring after the dew has dried. Dry them carefully in the shade or indoors. (A hint about drying leaves: the best method I have discovered is to place them on sweater racks. These are designed so that they can be stacked in tiers. Large quantities of leaves can be dried in the corner of the kitchen.)

Elder leaves added to salves made of beeswax and olive oil will be useful in healing bruises, sprains, wounds, and skin irritations. Prepare the salve and simmer the leaves on a low heat until the liquid turns green. Strain and bottle in brown glass jars.

The leaves boiled in linseed oil are an external remedy for hemorrhoids; taken internally they are purgative and diuretic. The juice is beneficial to eye inflammations.

Elder flower water is a traditional remedy to soothe sunburn pain and to clear skin blemishes. Fill a glass jar with the blossoms, pour boiling water over them (be careful to heat the jar first or it might crack), and add one and a half ounces of alcohol for each two quarts of water. Allow to steep for several hours, strain through a cheesecloth, bottle, and cork.

Elder flowers added to bath water are beneficial to the skin and soothing to the nerves. Infusing the dry flowers for an hour and straining off the liquid creates a soothing lotion for boils, tumors, and skin irritations.

Dry the flowers or tincture them in alcohol as a remedy for fevers, bronchitis, pneumonia, and measles. The infusion is an expectorant and a gentle laxative. Elder dilates the skin pores and promotes sweating. Remember to keep warm when a sweat is induced. Ideally, the patient should stay in bed well covered with wool blankets.

Elder flower tea is made in the spring and taken for several weeks on an empty stomach in the morning as a "spring tonic." It is also a good choice for colds and throat conditions. Elder and peppermint taken together are very helpful in the early stages of a flu. Yarrow may also be added to the brew. Cold elder flower tea benefits eye inflammations. (It is important that the tea is always strained through cheesecloth or a paper coffee filter before applying it to the eye.)

Eat the young elder buds after soaking them in hot water for a few minutes. Add oil, vinegar, and salt to make a salad that benefits skin eruptions. Elder flower vinegar eases a sore throat.

A salve comprised of the fresh flowers, beeswax, and olive oil is beneficial for burns, wounds, and chapped hands.

Infants and nursing mothers can benefit from the gifts of the Elder Mother. To create a soothing rub for sore nipples and breasts, cover dried elder flowers with olive oil and heat gently for about twenty minutes. Strain and cool. Elder blossom tincture is helpful for babies with fevers. Use one drop per pound of body weight either placed under the tongue or on the nipple of a nursing mother. It can be added to water and given by bottle to older children. Repeat as needed.

Elder Flower Vinegar

Cover one pound of dried elder flowers with one pint vinegar; seal and keep in a warm place for about eight days. Then strain through a coffee filter or gauze and store. This vinegar enhances salads too.

Elder Flower Pickle

Gather the buds of the flowers when green, cover with boiling vinegar, and seal when the vinegar has cooled.

Elderberries seem to clear the bone marrow and this results in a soothing effect for rheumatic pains. The berries also have a natural laetrile which may benefit or help prevent cancers.

Elderberries promote the movement of fluid secretions in the body, which helps to move lung congestion and clear blocked ears. (To enhance the effect, try adding a little fresh ginger root to the brew.) They also act as a gentle laxative. They are a classic remedy for bronchitis, colic, and diarrhea. When boiled in wine, the berries can help to induce late menstruation. (Elderberry root is the most powerful agent for this purpose.) A salve made from the green berries is helpful for hemorrhoids.

A pleasant way to promote a sweat is to drink Elderberry wine. It is also useful for the treatment of sore throats, phlegm, and chill. It is considered a prophylactic for flu. In addition, Elderberry wine or vinegar is an asthma remedy. To make the vinegar, cover the berries with apple cider vinegar for two weeks, shake occasionally, strain and store. Take in teaspoon doses as needed.

Elder Poultice

Inflammation of the joints can be relieved by simmering elder leaves, flowers, twigs, and bark with chamomile. Knead with slippery elm powder until the mixture is soft and has a pie-dough consistency.

Elderberry Cold Syrup

Ripe berries are simmered lightly in water with sliced ginger and whole cloves. Use about one ounce of ginger, eighteen cloves, and one quarter pound of berries. Cook for one hour, strain, bottle, and store in the refrigerator. In the event of a cold, add the syrup to a cup of hot water. Sweeten with honey if desired.

Elderberries are wonderful in pies, jams, jellies, muffins, custards, mousses, and as tea. One memorable pie was made by filling a shell with the berries, lemon, honey, and whipped egg whites. Delicious!

Apple and Elderberry Jam

> *3 lb. Elderberries*
> *3 lb. apples*
> *6 lb. sugar*
> *grated lemon peel and the juice of 3 lemons*

Boil the apples or the other fruit until soft and rub through a sieve. Add sugar and mix in a large pot. Boil until thick—about half an hour.

Elderberry Jam

> *1 cup fresh berries*
> *6 cups sugar*
> *liquid pectin*

Mash the berries with a potato masher and simmer about fifteen minutes. Add the sugar and stir until it has dissolved. Then add pectin. Boil for one minute, pour into jars and seal.

Caution: Be sure that you are using the berries of the Common Elder, *Sambucus canadensis*, or the Black Elder, *Sambucus nigra*. The elder family contains a type of Dwarf Elder, *Sambucus ebulus*, which has poisonous berries. Its roots are used in burn ointments and are reputed to clear the liver and the respiratory tract, and to promote urine and sweat. One teaspoon of the root is steeped in a cup of freshly boiled water and taken cold in mouthful doses of up to two cups per day. (This remedy is more drastic than the other elders and perhaps may not be suitable for ordinary household use.)

Black Elder (Sambucus Nigra) provides a homeopathic preparation used for coughs, sniffles, and asthma especially when these are accompanied by disturbances in the water balance of the body brought about by night sweats, watery stool, nephritis, and profuse urination and perspiration.

Magical Uses

The elder is an herb of Venus and is of the Water element. It is sacred to Venus, to Holda, and to the Great Goddess. It bestows powers of healing, protection, exorcism, prosperity, and wish manifestation.

Tradition holds that spirits of the forest enjoy inhabiting elder wood. Before cutting an elder, or taking any piece of it, it is wise to tell it of your intentions. Explain why you need the wood and make a suitable offering. This will give the Elder Mother time to vacate. Elder will seek revenge for any harm that comes to its trees.

Russian tradition states that out of compassion for all life, elder drives away evil spirits. The Germans and Scandinavians recognized Hylde-moer (Elder-Mother) or Hylde-vinde as a potent forest spirit who dwelled in elder trees.

During the middle ages, a person setting out on a journey would entrust their health and safety to a tree spirit. As long as the tree remained healthy and whole, so would the traveller, but if the tree became sick or died it was believed that the same fate would meet the traveller. These trees were known as Vard-trad or "guardian trees." In the old sailors' section of Copenhagen, each house had a protective elder tree.

To bring the blessing of the Elder Mother on a person, object, or place, her berries and leaves are scattered in the four directions and the person or object who is to receive the blessing is also showered with the leaves and berries.

Wearing elder protects an individual from physical or psychic attack, and when it is placed over the entrance of buildings it will prevent entry of negative energies. Grow it in your garden to bless and protect the house and land. To bring prosperity and good luck, elder is worn and used as a decoration at handfastings and weddings. Expectant mothers pay homage to the Elder Mother and ask it for blessings on the coming child.

Elderberries placed under your pillow help to dispel insomnia, and if worn in power bundles the berries curtail adulterous lust.

Elder branches have been traditionally used to make pan pipes and flutes because they are easily hollowed. Wood elves and spirits in distant glades respond to the sound of elder flutes.

Elder is a traditional wood for magic wands.

Every garden needs to have a wild place set aside especially for fairies and devas to use as a retreat—a place where animals and insects roam freely, but where no human dares to trespass. Any spot protected by an elder is especially blessed and a good candidate for such a sanctuary.

It is said that elder grants even the smallest wish, so use it with care. Never use the tree for selfish purposes or Elder Mother will balance your Karma more quickly than you may desire.

Meditating within a grove of elder trees facilitates communion with the woodland spirits. Approach the grove with reverence at the time of a full moon following a period of fasting. Midsummer Eve would be the best night.

Elder blossoms floated in a ritual cup are effective at magical rites. Elder flower water is good to use at child blessings and at baptism or "Wiccaning" ceremonies.

Elder is the tree of the last month (Ruis) of the Celtic calendar. Elder trees propagate easily and cuttings will readily put forth roots. She is the tree of life in death and of death in life. Even in the midst of apparent destruction she is capable of re-establishing herself anew. Use her to regenerate your life and your faith in times of hardship as you await rebirth.

Burn elder wood on the funeral pyre and bury it with the deceased as a protection and a blessing for the journey ahead.

Power Bundles

Trees can be incorporated into power bundles and medicine bags which can bring healing and transformation to the user. Simply refer to the index of "Magical Uses" in the back of this book and select the trees that have the qualities you need or desire.

For example, if you are seeking a new partner in life, a tiny piece of apple wood would be appropriate. Cedar might be added to strengthen your spiritual path, and oak to help make current projects more fruitful. Perhaps you want to improve your skills as a healer or are about to study massage; willow is a good choice for these. Plagued by lung problems? Select a small piece of eucalyptus for your bundle.

The bundle is created with the highest focus and intention that the practitioner can manage. Gather the woods with reverence and care, always leaving a gift for the tree such as a coin, a pinch of corn meal, or tobacco. Inform the tree of your gratitude by pouring libations of wine or cider on the roots.

You can "seal" the power in your bundle by making a mixture of cornmeal, corn pollen, flower pollens, earth, salt, Dragon's Blood (the herb), charcoal from a tree struck by lightning, sage, cedar needles, sweet grass, and lavender. Add a pinch of this mix to your bag along with a small crystal (such as a Herkimer diamond or a small double terminated quartz crystal) to amplify the energy. For healing, a tiny piece of turquoise is appropriate.

Add small carvings of totem animals or a bit of fur or feather from your "power animal." This will honor the animal and encourage it to manifest more fully in your life and work.

If these ideas seem obscure they are simply a reference to the common shamanic practice of divining an animal guide or helper and honoring its presence by dancing, singing, or creating effigies of the animal and working with them. Power animals are the equivalent of guardian angels from the animal kingdom. A person discovers their personal power animal by going into a trance with the aid of a drum and a rattle, or by going on a vision quest after fasting. Much can be learned about the health and psychic development of the individual from the actions of the animal helper.

Add anything to your bundle that would be symbolic for you as a power source—tiny statues of fairies, angels, or of the Goddess, even a statue of a saint would be appropriate.

Finally, add a part of yourself—hair clippings, nail parings, etc., anything that would add your personal signature to the blend.

Power bundles are worn for a year and a day after which they should be burned, buried in the earth, or cast to the waters.

Tree Meditation

This meditation works best any place where trees are growing. It is most effective within a circle of like-minded friends. Begin by orienting yourselves with the positions of the sun and moon. Note the four directions (north, east, south, and west) and their relation to your circle. Send a blessing and a prayer to the spirits of the four directions and thank them for their help and guidance.

When you feel you are attuned to the energies of the space in which you find yourselves, close your eyes. A spokesperson verbally guiding the process will help to keep everybody focused.

Start by becoming aware of your feet. Notice how they are resting on the earth. Begin to visualize them as extending and burrowing down into the soil. See clearly the taproots and tiny root hairs that curl and reach to anchor themselves in the soil. Notice your new awareness of earth energies, currents of magnetic power, and light. Notice also your awareness of the presence of water and of all the tiny organisms that feed and grow beneath you.

Leaving your "roots" firmly anchored, begin to raise your awareness to your trunk. Feel the sap coursing through your living wood and feel your sensitivity to the wind and sunlight. Now become aware of your highest branches. Feel your leaves turn and seek the light. The guide may direct the circle to raise their arms and wave their hands in sensitive, graceful motions to further capture the awareness of breezes and sun.

At this point some very startling things can occur. On a windless day in midwinter, I saw the trees around me begin to twist and move. There was a distinct crackling sound and I KNEW that they were communicating with us. Try it for yourself.

To end the meditation you simply reverse the process, retracting your leaves and branches and finally your roots.

Give thanks to the four directions and bless them for their help and presence.

Then, go forth with a new sensitivity to your friends, the trees.

Calendars & Alphabets

Tree calendars have their roots in the Goddess religions and the Tree Alphabet is a Gaelic development associated with the Celtic civilization. The Irish Tree alphabet was used until 700 A.D. For a detailed discussion of these please see Robert Graves' *The White Goddess* or Liz and Colin Murray's *The Celtic Tree Oracle.*

The Tree Calendar

Beith	Birch	November
Luis	Rowan	December
Fearn	Alder	January
Saille	Willow	February
Nuin	Ash	March
Huathe	Hawthorne	April
Duir	Oak	May
Tinne	Holly	June
Coll	Hazel	July
Quert	Apple	–
Muin	Vine	August
Gort	Ivy	September
Ngetal	Reed	October
Straif	Blackthorn	–
Ruis	Elder	Last 3 days of October

This calendar is a Lunar calendar with months being determined from moon to moon. Samhain, or Hallowe'en, marks the Celtic new year.

The Tree Alphabet

B	– Beith	– Birch
L	– Luis	– Rowan
N	– Nuin	– Ash
F	– Fearn	– Alder
S	– Saille	– Willow

H	– Huathe	– Hawthorn
D	– Duir	– Oak
T	– Tinne	– Holly
C	– Coll	– Hazel
M	– Muin	– Vine
G	– Gort	– Ivy
P or Ng	– Pethboc/Ngetal	– Dwarf Elder/Reed
R	– Ruis	– Elder
Q or CC	– Quert	– Apple
SS	– Straif	– Blackthorn
A	– Ailim	– Silver Fir
O	– Ohn	– Furze
U	– Ur	– Heather
E	– Eadha	– White Poplar
I	– Ioho	– Yew
Y	– (too sacred to have a written name)	– Mistletoe

Sources and Resources

Herbal

Audas, J.W.: *The Australian Bushland*. W.A. Hamer Pty. Ltd., North Melbourne, Australia, 1950.

Colby, Benjamin: *Guide to Health*. Morrill, Silsby, and Co., Concord, New Hampshire, 1845.

Culbreth, David: *A Manual of Materia Medica and Pharmacology*. Lea and Febiger, Philadelphia, Pennsylvania, 1927.

Culpeper, Nicholas: *Culpeper's Complete Herbal*. Richard Evans, London, England, 1814.

Grieve, M.: *A Modern Herbal*. Dover Publications, Inc., New York, 1982.

Hutchens, Alma. R.: *Indian Herbalogy of North America*. The Garden City Press Ltd., London, 1973.

Kneipp, Sebastian: *My Water Cure*. Jos. Koesel Publisher, Kempton, Bavaria, 1897.

Little, Edbert L.: *The Audubon Society Field Guide to North American Trees*. Alfred Al. Knopf Inc., New York, 1980.

Lust, John: *The Herb Book*. Benedict Lust Publications, Sini Valley, California, 1982.

Mathews, F. Schuyler: *Field Book of American Tress and Shrubs*. G.P. Putnam and Sons, New York and London, 1915.

Meyer, Joseph E.: *The Herbalist*. Clarence Meyer ed., Meyerbooks, Glenwood, Illinois, 1960.

Millspaugh, Charles F.: *American Medicinal Plants*. Dover Publications, Inc., New York, 1974.

Mitchell, Alan: *A Field Guide to the Trees of Britain and Northern Europe*. Collins, St. James Place, London, 1974.

Potterton, David ed.: *Culpeper's Color Herbal*. Sterling Publishing Co., Inc., New York, 1983.

Rogers, Julia Ellen: *The Tree Book*. Doubleday, Page and Co., New York, 1906.

Shook, Dr. Edward E.: *Advanced Treatise on Herbology*. Trinity Center Press, Beaumont, California, 1978.

Stewart, Hilary: *Cedar*. Douglas and McIntyre Ltd., Vancouver, British Columbia, Canada, 1984.

Weed, Susan S.: *Wisewoman Herbal For The Childbearing Year*. Ash Tree Publishing, Woodstock, New York, 1985.

Wyman, Donald: *Wyman's Gardening Encyclopedia*. Macmillan Pub. Co., New York, 1979.

Esculents (Edible Plants)

Clifton, Claire: *Edible Flowers*. McGraw-Hill Book Co., New York, 1984.

Crowhurst, Adrienne: *The Weed Cookbook*. Lancer Books Inc., New York, 1972.

Gibbons, Euell: *Stalking The Wild Asparagus*. David McKay Company Inc., New York, 1972.

Peterson, Lee Allen: *A Field Guide To Edible Wild Plants*. Houghton Mifflin Co., Boston, 1977.

Flower Essences

Bach, Edward: *Heal Thyself*. C.W. Daniel Co., Ltd., Saffron Walden, Essex, England, 1982.

Chancellor, Phillip M.: *Handbook of The Bach Flower Remedies*. C.W. Daniel Co., Ltd., Saffron Walden, Essex, England, 1982.

The Flower Essence Society, P.O. Box 459, Nevada City, CA 95959.

Dr. E. Bach Centre, Mount Vernon, Sotwell, Wallingford, Oxon, OX10 OPZ, England.

Homeopathy

Boericke, William: *Materia Medica with Repertory*. Boericke and Tafel, Philadelphia, Pennsylvania, 1927.

Standard Homeopathic Co., 210 W. 131st St., Box 61067, Los Angeles CA, 90061. (213) 321-4284.

The National Center For Homeopathy, 801 North Fairfax Street, Suite 306, Alexandria, Virginia 22314. (703) 548-7790.

Magic

Beyerl, Paul: *The Master Book of Herbalism*. Phoenix Publishing Co., Custer, Washington, 1984.

Cunningham, Scott: *Cunningham's Encyclopedia of Magical Herbs*. Llewellyn Publications, St. Paul, Minnesota, 1986.

Cunningham, Scott: *Magical Herbalism*. Llewellyn Publications, St. Paul, Minnesota, 1986.

Farrar, Janet & Stewart: *The Witches' Goddess*. Robert Hale Ltd., London, England, 1987.

Graves, Robert: *The White Goddess*. Creative Age Press, New York, 1948.

Matthews, Boris (translator): *The Herder Symbol Dictionary*. Chiron Publications, Wilmette, Illinois, 1986.

Murray, Alexander S.: *Manual of Mythology*. David McKay Publishers, Philadelphia, Pennsylvania, 1895.

Murray, Liz and Colin: *The Celtic Tree Oracle*. St. Martin's Press, New York, 1988.

Nitsch, Twylah Hurd: *Language of the Trees*. The Seneca Indian Historical Society, Irving, New York, 1982.

Porteous, Alexander: *Forest Folklore, Mythology and Romance*. MacMillan Co., New York, 1928.

Ross, Anne: *Pagan Celtic Britain*. Butler and Tanner Ltd., Frome and London, 1967.

For further information on Druids and the Druid path: Keltria, P.O. Box 33284, Minneapolis, MN 55443.

Index I   Herbal Uses

Abortion, herbal — cedar
Abscesses — apple
Acne — apple, walnut
Alcoholism — oak
Anti-bacterial — cedar
Antibiotics — apple
Antiscorbutic — pine (hemlock, Black Spruce)
Antiseptic — willow
Anxiety — poplar
Appetite — eucalyptus, walnut
Arterial tension — hawthorn
Arteries — holly
Arteriosclerosis — hawthorn
Arthritis — poplar, cedar
Asthma — eucalyptus, apple, elderberry
Asthma, in children — cedar
Athlete's Foot — apple

Babies, fever in — elder
Bad breath — oak
Baths — pine, apple, larch, walnut, elder
Baldness — birch
Bladder problems — pine, birch, apple, oak
Blisters — cedar
Bleeding, external — holly
Bleeding, internal — oak, willow
Bleeding, mucous membranes — pine, larch
Blood, to clean — apple
Blood circulation (to improve) — chestnut
Blood pressure, to lower — hawthorn
Blood pressure, to normalize — hawthorn
Blood vessels, to strengthen — pine
Bloody urine — oak
Boils — birch, elm, apple, walnut, elder, maple
Bone growths — apple

Bone necrosis — apple
Bowel, to clean — apple
Brain — elm, walnut
Breast milk, to dry — walnut
Breasts, sore — elder
Broken bones — holly, elm
Bronchitis — eucalyptus, elm, poplar, elder, pine
Bruises — pine, poplar, elder salve
Burns — willow, eucalyptus, elm, poplar, walnut

Calcium — elm
Calculi — apple
Cancer — walnut, elder
Carbuncles — apple
Catarrh — willow, holly, walnut
Cavities — apple
Chapped hands — elder
Chill, to ward off — elder
Chillblains — pine
Colds — holly, cedar, walnut, elder
Colic — holly, walnut, elder
Colitis — elm
Condylomata — cedar
Constipation — elm, walnut, oak, pine
Coronary artery — holly
Coughs — holly, elm, poplar, cedar, chestnut, pine, elderberry
Coughs, bloody — chestnut
Cystitis — elm, larch, pine, poplar

Dandruff — willow
Despair, hopelessness — chestnut
Diabetes, in children — hawthorn
Diarrhea — oak, willow, birch, elder, rowan, elm, apple, poplar, chestnut, larch, walnut, elderberry
Digestion — eucalyptus, apple, walnut (pickle), pine
Disinfectant — eucalyptus
Dislocated joints — holly
Distemper (in animals) — eucalyp-

tus
Diuretic — ash, elder, birch, holly, willow, cedar, larch
Dizziness — oak
"Doctrine of Signatures" — cedar, walnut
Douche — oak, rowan, walnut

Ears, blocked — elder, (ginger)
Eclectic school of medicine — walnut
Eczema — apple, birch, larch, walnut, ash
Emetic — holly
Emotion, upset — apple
Enema — elm, walnut
Energy — apple
Enteritis — elm
Erotomania — willow
Esculents (edibles) — acorn (oak), pine, ash, birch, maple, elm, rowan
Exhaustion — pine, eucalyptus
Expectorant — eucalyptus
Eye inflammations — elder
Eye problems — willow, maple, walnut, holly

Fasting — ash
Fear — poplar
Feeling overwhelmed — elm
Fever — oak, ash, elder, willow, chestnut, holly, walnut, birch, rowan, eucalyptus, apple, poplar, cedar, pine
Fibroids — ash
Fistulas and tumors of the rectal area — oak
Flower essences — oak, pine, willow, holly, chestnut, walnut, elm, larch
Flu — holly, eucalyptus, cedar, elder, walnut
Fluid secretions, to move — elder

Gangrene — elm, larch, willow
Gas pains — ash
Gastro-intestinal — eucalyptus
Gastritis — elm
Genito-urinary — eucalyptus, cedar

Germicide — apple
Glands, swollen — apple
Glandular inflammations — oak, walnut
Gleet — poplar
Goitre — oak
Gonorrhoea — willow, eucalyptus, poplar, cedar
Gout — ash, willow, birch, elm, apple, poplar, oak, rowan
Guilt — pine
Gum disease — eucalyptus, apple
Gums, sore — willow

Hemorrhoids — oak, elder, rowan, poplar, chestnut, walnut
Hair — apple, walnut
Hatred — holly
Headache — apple, poplar, elder, cedar, walnut
Head wounds — walnut
Heartbeat, irregular — hawthorn
Heartburn — willow, apple
Heart, feeble — hawthorn
Heart problems — eucalyptus, cedar, elder, hawthorn, (also yarrow, borage, motherwort, cayenne, dandelion)
Hemorrhages — larch, walnut, eucalyptus
Herpes (zoster) — maple
Hoarse voice — rowan, poplar
Homeopathy — oak, pine, willow, ash, hawthorn, rowan, eucalyptus, chestnut, cedar, poplar, walnut, elderberry, holly
Hunger, gnawing — pine
Hysteria — willow

Immune system — ash
Impetigo — elm
Indigestion — willow, apple
Infection, external — apple
Infection, internal — apple
Inflammations, external — apple, poplar
Influenza — eucalyptus
Insomnia — birch, hawthorn, elm, apple

Intermittent fever — oak
Intestines — chestnut, walnut
Intestines, to clean — apple
Intestines, to relax — poplar

Jealousy — holly
Jaundice — ash, poplar, walnut
Joints — elderberry

Kidney Problems — apple, elder, birch, pine, poplar

Labor, to promote — elder
Lack of confidence — birch
Laxative — ash, birch, rowan, apple, walnut, elder
Laetrile — elder
Leukemia — eucalyptus, oak
Liver cleanser — ash, maple, apple, poplar, walnut
Liver complaints — chestnut, larch
Lungs, bleeding — larch
Lung conditions — pine, holly, eucalyptus, elm, poplar, apple, chestnut
Lung congestion — oak, pine, eucalyptus, poplar
Lupus — apple

Malaria — eucalyptus
Manic depression — elm
Massage — pine, maple
Mastitis — elder
Mastoiditis — apple
Measles — elder
Melancholy, to relieve — larch
Menopause — walnut
Menstruation — cedar, birch, elder
Menstruation, excessive — larch
Mental arguments — chestnut
Milk substitute — elm
Mistakes repeated — chestnut
Mouth, infected — elder
Mouth sores — walnut
Mouth, sore — birch
Mucus congestion — elder
Mucus membranes — elm
Muscles, sore — pine
Myocarditis — hawthorn

Nausea — poplar
Nephritis — elderberry
Nervousness — hawthorn
Neuralgia — chestnut, elder
Nervousness — willow
Nightmares — poplar
Nightsweats — poplar, elderberry
Nipples, sore — elder
Nocturnal emissions — willow
Nymphomania — willow

Occipital pain — walnut
Oedema — apple, cedar, larch, birch, elder, hawthorn
Ophthalmia — apple
Ovarian pain — willow
Oversensitivity to changes — walnut

Pain relief — willow, poplar
Panic — poplar
Paralysis — apple
Piles — elder
Pleurisy — holly
Pneumonia — elder, eucalyptus
Poison Ivy — elm, birch
Poultice — elder, elm, birch
Psoriasis — apple, birch, larch
Puberty — walnut
Purgatives — holly, walnut, elder
Pyorrhea — eucalyptus

Quinine substitute — willow

Rectum, prolapsed — oak
Religious mania — poplar
Resentment, bitterness — willow
Rheumatic fever — hawthorn
Rheumatism — pine, ash, willow, holly, birch, elder, elm, apple, poplar, chestnut, cedar, rowan

Salves — poplar, walnut, elder
Salves, to make — see walnut
Satyriasis — willow
Scalp, itching of — walnut
Schizophrenia — walnut
Sciatica — apple, pine
Scrofula — walnut
Scurvy — pine, rowan, cedar

Index 2 Magical Uses

Index 3   Other Uses

About the Author

Ellen Evert Hopman is vice president of the Keltrian Druid order and has been teaching and practicing herbalism since 1983.

Her training began in the early seventies when she spent two summers foraging for wild foods and herbs near Woodstock, New York. Later she studied Flower Essence Counseling at the Findhorn Community in Scotland, apprenticed with Master Herbalist William Lesassier in New York City, and undertook the professional training course at the National Center for Homeopathy in Washington, D.C.

Her spiritual quest has led her to explore Zen meditation, T.M., Kundalini Yoga, Sufiism, Native American spirituality, Wicca, Christian mysticism, The Culdee Church of Ireland, Unitarian Universalism, Tantric practices and the Druid path. She holds an M.Ed. in Mental Health Counseling and maintains a holistic practice in western Massachusetts.

You may write to Ellen at:
Ellen Evert Hopman
P. O. Box 219
Amherst, MA 01004